MENDELSSOHN.

Felix Mendelssohn Bartholdy   Frankfurt d. 13 September 1842

See Page 183.

MENDELSSOHN.

LETTERS AND RECOLLECTIONS.

BY

DR. FERDINAND HILLER.

TRANSLATED,

WITH THE CONSENT AND REVISION OF THE AUTHOR,

BY M. E. VON GLEHN.

WITH AN INTRODUCTION BY

JOEL SACHS

NEW YORK
VIENNA HOUSE
1972

International Standard Book Number: 0-8443-0003-9
Library of Congress Catalogue Number: 70-163790
Manufactured in the United States of America

INTRODUCTION

Superficially, the nineteenth century was the "romantic era," the epoch of "inspiration," short-lived genius, and musical flower-pieces. It was also – and, on a large canvas, primarily – the era of music as a business. Music in the time of Queen Victoria became a commodity, to be sold to an immense and swelling audience. A climate of increasing intellectual bitterness, artistic feuding related to political ideologies, and struggles to win audiences and jobs, gave birth to personality cults, pamphleteering, and near-libellous personal attacks. Figures rose and fell – or were dragged down – and for each, memoirs abounded. The authenticity of these was often suspect; some were mere propaganda. Others, however, were awaited eagerly, for they had a claim to validity and were the products of men of distinction. Since none of the personality cults captured the English mind quite like that of Mendelssohn, their new Handel, no memoir would have been received with greater delight than that from one of Mendelssohn's closest friends. Reviewing the publication of *Letters and Recollections, The Musical Times* (December 1, 1874) expressed this with great enthusiasm:

We can scarcely imagine any person more thoroughly competent to place 'Letters and Recollections' of Mendelssohn before the world than Dr. Ferdinand Hiller; for both as an earnest artist and a sincere friend of the composer, he had frequent opportunities of closely observing not only the constant manifestations of his exceptional musical powers, but the many social qualities which endeared him to all who came within his influence

...there can be little doubt that any record of [the] delightful hours [that they spent together] must have the utmost interest for all who love the art to which they were devoted.

Ferdinand Hiller himself was no stranger to England at that time, having just recently appeared there, a man in his sixties and one of Germany's most distinguished pianists. He was born in 1811 to a wealthy Frankfurt merchant family that, like Mendelssohn's, was at home with the intellectual elite.[1] As a little boy he was briefly trained as a violinist, but far preferred studying piano with Aloys Schmitt (pianist, organist, and composer; 1788–1866), and harmony and counterpoint with Johann Georg Vollweiler (1770–1847). While Hiller introduces himself in *Letters and Recollections* with a modest comment that at ten he was known as the little pianoforte player with long hair, his precocity was at least as impressive as his rather modern appearance, for at that age he played Mozart's C-minor concerto in public and began to compose. This was also the time when he met Mendelssohn, who almost at once became his close friend. Like many talented young men of the middle class, Hiller was originally destined for a "learned" rather than a musical profession, but, in 1825, after his teacher Schmitt left Frankfurt, the fourteen-year-old boy journeyed to Weimar, with recommendations from Spohr and Moscheles, to study with Johann Nepomuk Hummel, one of the most renowned pianists and composers of the day, and one of Mozart's most

---

[1] For further biographical information see Reinhold Sietz's article in *Die Musik in Geschichte und Gegenwart*.

prized students. Hiller, in his vivid description of these years (*Künstlerleben*, 1880), indicates the powerful influence the celebrated composer and all the intellectuals of the town – including Goethe – had on his formation as a man of broad culture. He also relates that although he went to Weimar to study piano, the urge to compose overcame his desire to practice, so that lessons with Hummel gradually became lessons in composition.

While the pleasures of this time must have been wonderful enough for any boy of 16, undoubtedly the most exciting experience was Hiller's visit to Vienna with the Hummels in 1827, where he met Schubert and the dying Beethoven. Shortly thereafter, he left Hummel and returned home to Frankfurt. Then, in 1828, Hiller began a seven-year sojourn in Paris, again bearing letters of recommendation that assured his reception into the city's intellectual world. There he got to know all the leading musicians – Cherubini, Rossini, Meyerbeer, Berlioz, Chopin, Liszt, Kalkbrenner, Herz, Bellini, and many others, whose lives, crossing with Mendelssohn's, color *Letters and Recollections*. Furthermore, he travelled in a social circle that was by no means limited to musicians, and could count Delacroix, Victor Hugo, and Heinrich Heine among his friends. Intimacy was sufficient with some (ee.gg. Mendelssohn, Liszt) to warrant the use of "tu". Like many of his generation, Hiller tirelessly exerted himself to propagate the music of earlier composers, introducing Paris to the "Emperor" concerto, and, with Chopin and Liszt, performing a three-"piano" concerto of J. S. Bach.

After spending the year 1836–1837 conducting

the Cæcilia Society in Frankfurt, Hiller visited Milan, where he wrote an opera, *Romilda*, on a libretto suggested by Rossini. (Its production at La Scala in 1839 was marked by a singular lack of success.) He then completed his oratorio *Die Zerstörung Jerusalems*, encouraged by Mendelssohn, who conducted it in Leipzig in 1840. A second Italian journey, during which he married, gave Hiller an opportunity to study the music of Palestrina. In the mid-1840's, residing in Leipzig, Frankfurt, and Dresden, he became a close friend of the Schumanns (the A-minor piano concerto is dedicated to him) and violinists Joseph Joachim and Ferdinand David. Unfortunately, in 1843 his friendship with Mendelssohn abruptly ended, apparently (at least according to Liszt) because Mendelssohn expressed strong reservations about Mme. Hiller's ability to sing publicly.[2] Later in the decade a much shorter and far less intimate friendship, between Hiller and Wagner, also terminated.

In 1847 Hiller accepted a post as municipal Kapellmeister in Düsseldorf, and three years later one in Cologne. There he settled, reorganizing the conservatory and becoming its director – a position he filled nearly to the end of his life. The most famous of his many students over the next 30-odd years was Max Bruch.

Hiller now became one of the most influential men in German musical life, conducting the Lower

---

[2] See Reinhold Sietz, "Vier unbekannte Briefe F. Mendelssohns an F. Hiller," *Mitteilungen der Arbeitsgemeinschaft für rheinische Musikgeschichte*, No. 3 (1955), and Eric Werner, *Mendelssohn: A New Image of the Composer and his Age*, trans. Dika Newlin (New York: Free Press of Glencoe, 1963), p. 392.

Rhine Festivals when they were held in Cologne, and writing frequently in the *Kölnische Zeitung*. His positions brought him into contact with all of musical Europe – the friendly correspondence with Verdi (1877–1884) is only one example – and in all his work his conservative inclinations were very pronounced. During the Cologne years he also continued to compose, and toured extensively as a pianist and conductor, visiting Russia, France, England, and the major European musical centers, nearly losing his job in Cologne as a result of his extended absences. Hiller resigned his posts in 1884 because of ill health, and died the following year, an old and successful man in the century of tragic endings.

As a pianist, Hiller was generally admired. Unlike the performing composers of the previous generation (such as Hummel), he continued throughout his life to play the music of others, acquiring great fame as an interpreter of Mozart and Beethoven; at the same time he was, like Hummel, a superb improvisor. His conducting, on the other hand, provoked very mixed reactions, inspiring enthusiasm tempered by a feeling in some quarters that his performance lacked passion. (Any judgments about performers must be accepted with great caution, however. Performing styles have always been so diverse that to cite Liszt condemning Hiller for a lack of passion – as is done in *MGG* – without taking into account Liszt's flamboyant personality would be grossly misleading.)

Hiller the composer was unquestionably one of the most prolific and versatile of a century that tended to produce specialists. Comprising some 200 works, his published *œuvre* includes operas, oratorios, dozens of songs and part-songs *(a cappella* and accompanied by piano or orchestra), symphonies, concertos, overtures, all manner of chamber music, and piano works ranging from salon-pieces to sonatas. Every aspect of nineteenth-century musical thought seems represented. The very titles of various piano pieces suggest Hiller's kinship with the major figures of his generation: Op. 158, *Forms from the Middle Ages* (character pieces with such titles as "The Knight," "The Nun," "The Minnesinger," "The Pilgrim," etc.), exhibits the spiritual inclinations of Liszt, the medievalism of so many *literati,* and the pictorialism of Schumann, Liszt, and countless others; dance suites and deliberately archaic contrapuntal works (e.g. the fugal etude of Op. 15) remind one of Hiller's interest in baroque and classical styles, which he and Mendelssohn did so much to resuscitate; the many Etudes show him in the company of Chopin and super-virtuosi like Thalberg and Kalkbrenner. Operas, oratorios, symphonies – Hiller, like his contemporaries, tackled all, aspiring to equal the successes of earlier masters.

Unfortunately, Hiller's compositions had, by and large, very mixed success. As a young man he showed such tremendous promise, that Chopin (referring to a symphony and concerto) called him "a man of the same type as Beethoven – full of poetry, fire, and soul."[3] Yet Hiller did not have the consistent mastery one sees in his better-remembered contem-

[3] *Correspondance de Frédéric Chopin,* ed. Bronislas Sydow *et. al.* (3 vols.; Paris, 1953–1960), Vol. II, p. 43. See p. 208, n. 224 for an account of how Chopin told Hiller of his first (and negative) reaction to George Sand.

poraries. Schumann, reacting to the Op. 15 Etudes, found among them some of the best piano music "since Beethoven's Sonata in F minor [Op. 57] and certain pieces of Franz Schubert" and things "I would not for anything have allowed to be printed."[4] Schumann's instinct proved ultimately to be correct. An unevenness in Hiller's music seems to justify the self-deprecatory remarks that permeate the unseen half of the Hiller-Mendelssohn correspondence, projected to the reader by Mendelssohn's frequent words of advice and encouragement.

Hiller's best works seem to be those for piano. Like Mendelssohn's, they are frequently very brilliant, or consist predominantly of slowly-moving melodies supported by extremely active accompaniments. The Etudes, Op. 15, show him at his most interesting: there is a compactness of ideas (as in Chopin's Etudes), a refreshing unpredictability of treatment, and a clean, transparent texture that often – but not always – implies well thought-through voice-leading. Hiller's music is typically "right-handed", but lacks the exploitation of colors characteristic of his friend Liszt. Alas, here and there in the Etudes – and in many other compositions – positive qualities are neutralized by an inability to sustain interest and a tendency to lapse into rather bookish developmental procedures. In short, Hiller often falls into the common post-Beethoven trap: he self-consciously yearns to master the honored technique of motivic unification, but is instinctively drawn to long melodies that are not suited to development.

[4] Leon Plantinga, *Schumann as Critic* (New Haven: Yale University Press, 1967), p. 231.

Hiller produced nearly as much vocal as instrumental music. His songs and part-songs reveal him in a more intimate vein. Unlike the accompaniments of Liszt's songs, Hiller's are rarely difficult; texture and vocal style follow the tradition of Schubert and have little in common with the almost operatic virtuosity of many mid-century *Lieder*. Some of the songs are sadly disfigured, however, by texts of an insipid bourgeois sentimentality, which sometimes led Hiller to harmonies of an all-too-purple character.

Of the larger works, the oratorios were the most famous, particularly *Die Zerstörung Jerusalems,* which is discussed in *Letters and Recollections.* While the operas, like the symphonies, were never well known, *Die Zerstörung Jerusalems* was considered one of the best efforts in a popular and conservative genre.

Hiller's conservative persuasion is clearly articulated in his many literary works, all of which bear the stamp of a fine writer and truly cultivated man. Touching upon nearly every important aspect of musical life, from conducting by memory to a beautiful eulogy of Schumann, they make, along with Hiller's correspondence,[5] a splendid entrée into the bubbling musical cauldron of the better part of a century. They are works of a man who regards the past with pride and retains as much of it as he can. In a characteristic passage *(Künstlerleben,* p. 16), Hiller says, almost wistfully, that Hummel had the virtue of representing a generally-valid direc-

---

[5] Published as *Aus Ferdinand Hillers Briefwechsel,* ed. Reinhold Sietz (6 vols.; *Beiträge zur rheinischen Musikgeschichte,* Nos. 28, 48, 56, 60, 65, 70 [Cologne, 1958–1968]).

tion; "Nowadays," he laments, "we live in experiments." The ease and clarity with which Hiller presents his point of view is even more striking when compared with Wagnerian verbosity.

∽✻∾

One cannot say with certainty how long Hiller contemplated a book about Mendelssohn. He hardly lacked raw material, for, as the reader will notice, the book consists more of letters than recollections. Hiller was well aware of the need for a book sympathetic to his old friend, for by the 1860's he was regularly called upon to defend his own music, outlook, and Jewish ancestry against the same attacks levelled at Mendelssohn by "progressives." And this had been going on for some years. A letter to Hiller from a Frau Brückmann (Paris, 1861) begins with the complaint, "What would Mendelssohn have said to the Wagner rubbish in Germany!...Even in the last years of his life the Leipzig clique had already begun to raise its head. As I spoke to him for the last time [a few days before his death] he lamented to me about how much Leipzig musical life had changed since my stay there nine years earlier."[6] That the insults of his former friend Wagner were particularly galling, is apparent in Hiller's response to "Über das Dirigiren", in which he treated Wagner with the utmost contempt, scornfully addressing him as a self-proclaimed god (Kölnische Zeitung, April 14, 1870). It was two decades since Wagner's notorious attack on Jews in music in the Neue Zeitschrift

---

[6] Ibid., Vol. II, p. 183. Translation by this author.

für Musik, but the hair of the German Jews was still standing on end, and although Hiller does not often mention his origins, in *Künstlerleben* he shows clearly his sensitivity about being Jewish.

Hiller's contact with Mendelssohniana had been renewed in 1863, when he reviewed the newly-published Mendelssohn family letters. He may therefore have been further stimulated to write a book when, in December 1872, he received an invitation to write the article on Mendelssohn for the *Allgemeine deutsche Biographie.* While he did not accept the commission, *Letters and Recollections* must have been begun shortly afterwards (if it was not already under way). By the summer of 1873 Hiller was putting the final touches on it (the foreword is dated September, 1873); the Cologne firm of Dumont-Schauberg released it in 1874. About the time of its completion, George Grove wrote Hiller to offer, on behalf of Macmillan's, £50 for the English copyright; they would print it serially in *Macmillan's Magazine* (a monthly treating politics, travel, the arts, philosophy, etc.), and subsequently as a book. All expenses, including those of translation, were to be borne by the company.[7] The translator, M. E. von Glehn, was, incidentally, a "Miss", one of the many ladies who, following no full-time career, must have had ample leisure to cultivate languages and were often busy as translators.

The English version of *Letters and Recollections* appeared in five installments, commencing January, 1874; some of the letters also appeared slightly later, without Hiller's commentary, in *The Mu-*

---

[7] For further details see *ibid.,* Vol. III. *Macmillan's Magazine* had published eight letters of Mendelssohn in 1871.

sical World. After some minor revisions and the addition of prefaces and the dedication, Miss von Glehn's translation was published as the book presented here in a reprint edition.[8] The dedication to Queen Victoria is a touching tribute to the connections between Mendelssohn and England, and Germany and the English crown. Hiller may have obtained permission for the dedication during his trip to England in 1872; whether Victoria rewarded him for the dedication, as had been traditional, is unknown. In any event, since Victoria and Albert had known Mendelssohn and even made music with him in 1842 (Albert playing the organ and Victoria, who was also a talented pianist, singing songs by Felix and his sister Fanny),[9] the Queen certainly must have received the gesture warmly.

One question Hiller did not leave unanswered was that of his intentions in bringing forth the book. In the Preface he wrote, "Now, however, I come forward all the more boldly with these pages . . . because [Mendelssohn], one of the brightest and most beautiful stars in the firmament of German art, is experiencing, in his own country, the attacks of envy, of want of comprehension and judgment, which can only bring dishonour on those from whom they proceed, for they will never succeed in detracting from the glory which surrounds his name. Gold cannot be tarnished" (p. xxxi). While Hiller leaves further clarification tactfully tacit, the preface to the French edition (Paris, 1877), provides

---

[8] A second German edition was published in 1878; concerning the French version (Paris, 1877), see below.

[9] Werner, *op. cit.,* p. 382.

its readers with superabundant enlightenment. In fact, the translator, Félix Grenier (a lawyer, civil servant, and trained composer and pianist) had so much to say that with effort he condensed his thoughts into an "avant-propos du traducteur" of 93 pages – one fourth of the entire book. Grenier tells his readers of the envy and fanaticism of coteries in Germany and France whose sole purpose was to denigrate Mendelssohn. In both countries these groups were hiding behind powerful names – A. B. Marx and Wagner in Germany, F. J. Fétis and Félix Clément in France. Grenier dismisses Wagner's "Das Judenthum in der Musik" as a contemptible manifestation of "amour propre" and excessive pride, although he grants Wagner musical genius, reminding the reader all the same that genius is the brother of madness. As for the others, Grenier demolishes their attacks on Mendelssohn's character and the errors of fact (particularly in Fétis' article on Mendelssohn in the *Biographie Universelle*), presenting the testimony of others to refute any suggestions that Mendelssohn was one bit less than noble. Clément's discussion of Mendelssohn (in *Les musiciens célèbres depuis le xvie siècle jusqu'à nos jours*) was so bad that it might have been ignored, snaps Grenier, were it not destined for young readers and thus all the more dangerous. This irate defense of Mendelssohn is most eloquent, and by its very length and fury testifies to the seriously precarious position of the dead composer's reputation.[10] The three pages in conclusion

---

[10] Werner treats the fate of Mendelssohn's reputation in his final chapter.

about Hiller seem anti-climactic, but Hiller was probably too well known to have needed more.

❧

Letters and Recollections is a true period-piece, whose flavor is far from lost in translation. The very floridness of the English version's Victorian language captures the spirit not only of Hiller's attitudes toward his friend, but also of the quality of "renaissance man" which the literary-minded English admired in both of them. There is, however, far more than a pleasing spirit to the book, as *The Musical Times* recognized:

It would be impossible, with the few quotations we could give from the letters in this volume, to convey the faintest idea of the rich contents of the book. Dr. Hiller is an accomplished literary man, as well as a distinguished musical artist; and the style with which he relates his experiences is exceedingly attractive, apart from the interesting matter upon which he treats. His veneration for his deceased friend is so thoroughly shared in by the world at large that even the minute points of character which he occasionally enlarges upon, will be interesting to the majority of his readers.

Indeed, as Mendelssohn's biographer Eric Werner points out, Hiller is one of the best sources of information about Mendelssohn's personal life, since the two sometimes lived together, and "concerning his musical associations in Paris, we learn more from Hiller than from any other source."[11] (The sense of intimacy conveyed by Mendelssohn's use of "Du" is unfortunately lost in translation.)

---

[11] Werner, pp. 188 and 335.

Furthermore, the book's usefulness is hardly limited to Mendelssohn. Through the eyes of Hiller – always the modest observer – we see the world of the great Romantic generation. Even allowing for poetic license or errors resulting from the long elapsed time between an event and its description, one cannot help feeling the extraordinary presence of this period in passages such as that on page 25: "I remember that one day, Mendelssohn, Chopin, Liszt, and I, had established ourselves in front of a café on the Boulevard des Italiens...." The thought of these four young men, hardly more than teenagers, lounging over a cup of coffee and watching Parisian traffic, with perhaps no one knowing who they were or what three of them would mean to future generations, has an odd sense of unreality – an earthiness somehow inappropriate to immortal souls. The same can be said of Hiller's tale of how he and Mendelssohn would skip lunch to save more room for French pastries in the late afternoon.

The strong sense of presence also gives Hiller's book a matchless force in driving home the picture of a closely intertwined musical world. Any reader who begins by naïvely assuming that these musicians existed independent of one another, apart from those influences transmitted by hearing one another's works, will have an eye-opening, as he learns how one composer would arrange work for another, write to a publisher on behalf of a friend, or provide a scarce score for a performance. There are also many intriguing, if not wholly objective, descriptions of concerts and audiences in various German cities, and a wealth of information about private musical life, such as the amusing account of Hiller playing the "Emperor" concerto for a house party, accompanied by a string quartet, with wind parts provided by Mendelssohn on a second piano, "from memory" (p. 29). It is, in short, a whole epoch, with Mendelssohn at the focal point.

∽❧∾

Letters and Recollections was, as far as can be determined, a great success. Hiller's extant communications include many flattering references to the book (even one from the Countess d'Agoult, former mistress of his friend Liszt and Wagner's mother-in-law). The vituperative preface to the French edition had at least one repercussion, however: in 1880, the son of the great French violinist Pierre Baillot (1771–1842) wrote to protest the inclusion of somewhat irrelevant comments by Spohr expressing disdain for the elder Baillot's playing. In view of the thoroughly tactful atmosphere of the book – the names of Mendelssohn's detractors are not mentioned – it seems likely that Hiller had not known the contents of the preface in advance.[12]

After the Mendelssohn book, Hiller's career as a writer for the English audience seemed only to be beginning. Even while the memoir was still being serialized, Grove was again pen-in-hand, requesting contributions to the dictionary of music that he was editing for Macmillans: "Your Mendelssohn is so charming and has made so many people talk, that your help in my Dictionary will be naturally looked on and it will never do to put you to small names or

---

[12] Pointed out by Sietz, *Briefwechsel,* Vol. IV, pp. 123–125.

inferior articles."[13] Hiller was not, however, about to be tempted: of the many "large" names – including Mendelssohn – he finally chose to write only about Ferdinand David; the Mendelssohn article fell to Grove himself. Otherwise, Hiller's last contribution to England was an article on Cherubini in *Macmillan's Magazine* the following year. In view of the charm of his style, it is sad that he could not be induced to write more, but he was, after all, one of Germany's most active musicians to the end of his days.

In the long run, *Letters and Recollections,* for all the aroused hopes that it might teach some sense to Mendelssohn's enemies, was only a way-station in the bitter conflict that resulted in Germany's banning Mendelssohn's music in the 1930's. Perhaps it is therefore all the more appropriate that the book now be available again, nearly a century after its first publication. With Mendelssohn's star again on the rise he may now (as Hiller concludes) be "honored and praised as a chosen favorite of Apollo and the Muses."

JOEL SACHS

Columbia University
July 15, 1972

---

[13] *Ibid.,* Vol. III, pp. 140ff.

CONCERNING THE TEXT

Reinhold Sietz, who has had access to the originals of Mendelssohn's letters, has been able to supply the names for which Hiller left blank spaces in the book, and certain passages that he suppressed (probably to spare the feelings of the people cited). Sietz's list, printed in *Mitteilungen der Arbeitsgemeinschaft für rheinische Musikgeschichte*, No. 2 (Cologne, 1955), pp. 25–26, is reproduced below, translated by this author. In addition, five letters from Mendelssohn which Hiller decided to omit were published by Sietz in *Aus Ferdinand Hillers Briefwechsel (Beiträge zur rheinischen Musikgeschichte*, No. 28 [Cologne, 1958], pp. 33–34, and "Vier unbekannte Briefe F. Mendelssohns an F. Hiller", *Mitteilungen der Arbeitsgemeinschaft für rheinische Musikgeschichte*, No. 3 (Cologne, 1955) pp. 38–40.

Page 45, line 9: Leo

Page 63, line 8 and following: Wilhelm Schadow

Page 63, line 17: Stephanie Nesselrode

Page 65, line 6: St. George

Page 66, line 18: *For* the three dots *read* Schlemmer will certainly never be the same again. Yesterday I learned of the death of old Rothschild and certainly this will also have a lot of influence on his whole existence. It is a very sad event for the family, and has truly distressed me; I wish you would write me something about this, and tell me in particular if you can get wind of what Schlemmer will do, if he will stay there or not, and what then. I am greatly interested to know something about it.

Page 66, line 18: St. George

Page 67, line 9: *After* burn it *read* and show it to no one

Page 69, line 12: Schadow

Page 74, line 7 from bottom: Passavant

Page 76, line 5: Schumann

Page 80, line 5: (Louise) Hetsch, (Joseph) Strauss

Page 80, line 8 from bottom: *For* etc... *read* i.e. (Franz) Lachner.

Page 84, line 10: *After* discussions *read* the most lively recently at night by the Main, with Schlemmer and his brother,

Page 86, line 12: *After* heart *read* I have given Hofmeister your instructions, but he says that he has already sent you the desired Etudes and Caprices, and I have commissioned the brother of my bride to deliver the 3 Florins to you. Pardon my error, but you had written me on your ticket that I should receive 60 Prussian Thaler from you, and since, as you know, I have never become clever, I knew nothing else, and stuck to your ticket.

Page 97, line 5 from bottom: (Ferdinand) Ries

Page 101, line 10 from bottom: *After* counterpoint *read* at the tenth

Page 104, line 13: Hummel...Weimar

Page 108: *As postscript* Cécile keeps wanting me to greet you from her, separately. I do this hereby, and want to do it just as nicely as she demands.

Page 118, line 7: Meyerbeer

Page 119, line 8: Reissiger

Page 120: *As postscript* Let me know really a lot about the Italian operas and theaters, that is really too interesting. Above all, however, how far you are with yours.

Page 121, line 9 from bottom: *For* your Italian life *read* your grand Italian opera

Page 125, line 6 from bottom: (Karl) Voigt

Page 125, line 5 from bottom: (Xaver) Schnyder von Wartensee

Page 131, line 9: *After* oratorio *read* about Elijah

Page 132, line 8: (Gottfried W.) Fink

Page 143, line 9: *After* doings *read* I would only like you to write another opera immediately, and then another—through that would be your own personal goal, "to promote yourself right in the field" be fulfilled, and that they must prevail through all that wilderness of stupidity and arrogance among musicians and the public, that is as clear to me as the sun. I wish you would do it.

Page 148, line 13: *After* you. *read* When you wrote me a few lines, tell me if you need the second part of your Oratorio now. I have made various notes about it, but don't know if I should send it to you at this time and am almost afraid that wouldn't be convenient for you.

Page 195, lines 1, 16 and 5 from bottom: Schlesinger

Page 195, line 4: *After* if you like *read* and you are not otherwise disposed about the sonata,

Page 195, line 5 from bottom: Trautwein

Page 199, line 2 from bottom: (Heinrick K.) Schleinitz

Page 203, line 3: (Heinrich) Neeb

TO THE QUEEN.

MADAM,

The great nation which has the happiness of living in the freedom of the law under your Majesty's glorious sceptre shows its continuous mental relationship to the people of Germany, who owe their origin to the same race, in nothing perhaps more plainly than in the ardour with which for upwards of a century it has appropriated the creations of our great composers. Just as Shakespeare has become to the Germans a national poet, so to the English is Handel a national composer. The immortal works of Mozart, Beethoven, Haydn, and Weber met with enthusiastic reception and lasting admiration in England, as did Haydn and Weber themselves. But it was genuine affection which the people of

Britain bestowed upon our great and youthful master, Felix Mendelssohn Bartholdy. Hardly more than a boy when he began his artistic career in London, he soon won all hearts. Everyone watched with fond and eager interest the steady progress of the youth and the man whose greatest work, his "Elijah," the ripest fruit of his genius, was first presented to the world at an English festival. He well deserves the honour bestowed upon him of a place amongst the chosen spirits whose portraits adorn the monument which Your Majesty, as a wife and as a Queen, has erected to a Prince who occupies so prominent a position amongst the noblest promoters of human culture.

The rare distinction bestowed upon this little book, of being allowed to bear the victorious name of Your Majesty, is due above all to the memory of the glorious master to whom it is consecrated. My thanks are doubly heartfelt.

May a reflection of the gracious reception which
my noble friend enjoyed from Your Majesty be
granted to the following pages, consecrated as
they are to his memory, and also partly ema-
nating from him.

I have the honour to subscribe myself,

Madam,

Your Majesty's humble and devoted servant,

FERDINAND HILLER.

PREFACE.

PHOTOGRAPHY often gives us the most different likenesses of the same man, each one recognizable, but none exhaustive; and it is only the painter provided he be a real artist—who, out of the manifold reflections photographed on his brain, can produce a portrait in which everyone may read what he himself saw in the original, and which everyone will acknowledge to be a representation of the *whole* man. In the same way the traits which different people seize in giving their personal recollections of a famous man will always be somewhat one-sided, in spite of the most truthful intention, and it is only the biographer—and he the right one—who, by putting everything together, all that he has seen and heard, or even guessed, can bring to light

the individuality of the man, in all its completeness and fulness of meaning. Even in
letters and conversations, where everyone depicts
himself, there is a certain photographic one-sided-
ness, because they are intended only for a single
individual; and most people, however true they
may be to themselves, always modify their mental
physiognomy to a certain extent, according to the
different individualities with which they come
into contact. I have endeavoured in these pages
to give a picture of Mendelssohn as he is reflected
in my remembrance; they may therefore, perhaps,
supply material to his future biographer, giving
as they do a new aspect of that richly-gifted
man, or at any rate, a more complete picture of
one side of him than has hitherto been supplied
to us in the valuable writings and letters already
published, namely, in his relations to a true-
hearted artist-friend and comrade, if I may be
allowed thus to style myself. The peculiarity
of his relations to me, even at the early age at
which his genius had ripened and he became
celebrated, was, that they were those not only

of friendly affection, but of real fellowship. I
very much regret that I was not in the habit
of putting down my experiences, during the
years in which, from time to time, I enjoyed
such intimate intercourse with him. Many precious
details have escaped me, though I still have a
perfectly clear picture of my friend before me.
However, all that I have told may be received
with the most implicit confidence.

Music cannot be described; language is totally
incapable of giving even the most distant idea
of a musical composition. And in the same
way, very little can be told of the actual communications which go to make up the intimate
intercourse of two musicians. The hours which
I spent with Mendelssohn at the piano, in
the interchange of our views on music and
compositions of all kinds, our own and other
people's, were, in a certain sense, the best which
I had the happiness of enjoying with him; but
it would be impossible for me to give more than
the most general account of them. If, on the
other hand, I have tried to preserve many of my

dear friend's remarks, that are perhaps trivial, or insignificant traits of speech or action, I have done so with the conviction that the merest trifle is interesting, when a great man is concerned. Mendelssohn's admirers have reproached me for not coming forward long ago with my communications. Various reasons withheld me, and one above all others, namely, that I might not give occasion to the very slightest accusation of trying to gain popularity through his friendship. Proud of it as I was and am, it was too sacred to me to be made use of. Now however, I come forward all the more boldly with these pages, so full of admirable traits of the departed, because he, one of the brightest and most beautiful stars in the firmament of German art, is experiencing, in his own country, the attacks of envy, of want of comprehension and judgment, which can only bring dishonour on those from whom they proceed, for they will never succeed in detracting from the glory which surrounds his name. Gold cannot be tarnished.

Thus, with fond devotion, I add this simple

EDITOR'S PREFACE.

My part in this work has been confined to the pleasant task of passing an excellent translation through the press, and adding a few notes of date or place to the text, since its appearance in "Macmillan's Magazine."

The volume has had the advantage of Dr. Hiller's revision, and for this and his permission to make use of the portrait, the best thanks of the publishers and myself are due to him.

As a lover of music and of Mendelssohn, however, I owe him a much deeper debt, which I gladly acknowledge. This book is undoubtedly the most important contribution to the biography of Mendelssohn that has appeared since the publication of the two volumes of his Letters. One more volume of letters to his family, or one more

like the present, but addressed to a non-musician—
a Schubring or a Hildebrandt—and, whether his
Life be ever written or not, the world would
be in tolerably full possession of one of the
most remarkable, interesting, and many-sided
characters of the century.

As I write the news arrives of the death of
Paul Mendelssohn, Felix's younger brother, and
the last remaining member of the family circle to
which he was so fondly attached. It is a double
reminder—first that but for over-work and over-
excitement Felix Mendelssohn himself might have
been still with us, or but recently departed; and
secondly that those who knew him personally, and
to whom he was not only a musician but a living,
loving friend, rich beyond measure in the gifts
and powers of life, are fast passing away with
their recollections and traditions out of the reach
of the biographer.

G. GROVE.

SYDENHAM,
     June 25th, 1874.

CONTENTS.

PRINCIPAL DATES IN MENDELSSOHN'S LIFE.

1809. Born at Hamburg, Feb. 3.

1815 or 16. Family remove to Berlin. Becomes Zelter's pupil.

1821. First visit to Goethe.

1822. Tour in Switzerland.

1825. Octett. Trumpet Overture. Journey to Paris and Cherubini.

1826. Overture to Midsummer Night's Dream.

1828. Overture, Meeresstille.

1829. First visit to London. Tour in Scotland.—Reformation Symphony.

1830-1. Third visit to Goethe. Italian journey.—Hebrides Overture : Italian Symphony : Walpurgis-night.

1832. Munich, Paris, London. G minor Concerto.

1833-4. Düsseldorf. London. Overture to Melusine. St. Paul.

1835. Düsseldorf. Leipsic. Death of his father, Nov. 19.

1836. Leipsic. Frankfort.—Betrothal. St. Paul first performed, May 22.

1837. Marriage, March 28. D minor Concerto. 42nd Psalm. Birmingham.

1838. Leipsic.—Serenade and Allegro giojoso—E flat Quartet.

1839. Leipsic.—Ruy Blas. D minor Trio. Many Songs.

1840. Leipsic. England.—Festgesang. Lobgesang.

1841. Leipsic. Berlin.—Antigone. Scotch Symphony. Variations Sèrieuses. First illness.

1842. Berlin. Leipsic. London, with his wife. Switzerland. Death of his mother, Dec.

1843. Leipsic, Berlin.—Midsummer Night's Dream Music. Athalie. Psalms.

1844. Berlin. London. Soden.—Violin Concerto. C minor Trio. Overture to Athalie. Organ Sonatas.

1845. Berlin. Frankfort.—Œdipus. B flat Quintet. Elijah begun. Resigns post at Berlin.

1846. Leipsic. Elijah at Birmingham, Aug. 25. Lauda Sion.

1847. Leipsic. London. Switzerland. Death of his sister Fanny, May 14. Christus. Loreley. F minor Quartet. Death Nov. 4.

CHAPTER I.

IN the summer of 1822 I was living in my native town of Frankfort—beautiful Frankfort— and, though barely eleven, was just beginning to be known in the town as "the little pianoforte player with the long hair." The long hair was the best known thing about me, I think, for it was very long; still, I had actually played in public once, which my school-fellows thought a great wonder. I had been taught the piano by Aloys Schmitt, in a very irregular fashion, for he was always travelling; but he was fond of me, and I had quite a passion for him. The winter before, Schmitt had been in Berlin, and on his return told us of a wonderful boy, a grandson of Moses Mendelssohn the philosopher, who was not only a splendid player, but had composed quartets, symphonies, operas! Now I had composed too— Polonaises and Rondos, and Variations on " Schöne Minka," which I thought extremely brilliant; and

B

I worked most diligently at harmony and counterpoint, under the venerable Vollweiler. But that a
boy only two or three years older than myself,*
should be conducting his own operas, seemed to
me unheard of. True, I had read the same thing
about Mozart; but then it was Mozart, and he was
more a demigod than a musician. So I was not
a little excited when Schmitt came to us one day
with the news that Felix Mendelssohn was in
Frankfort, with his father, mother, brother, and
sisters, and that he, Schmitt, would bring him to
see us the next day.

The house in which we lived really consisted
of two—one tolerably modern, looking on to the
river, and the other, an older one, adjoining the
first, and facing a narrow street, which contained
the only entrance to both. The windows at the
back of the modern house overlooked the court,
and one of them commanded the narrow passage
leading from it to the house door. At this window
I took my stand at the hour which Schmitt had
named for his visit, and, after waiting for some
time in the greatest impatience, was rewarded by
seeing the door open and my master appear. Behind him was a boy, only a little bigger than
myself, who kept leaping up till he contrived to

---

* Mendelssohn was born on the 3rd of February, 1809, and Hiller on
the 24th October, 1811.—*Ed.*

get his hands on to Schmitt's shoulders, so as to hang on his back and be carried along for a few steps, and then slip off again. "He's jolly enough," thought I, and ran off to the sitting-room to tell my parents that the eagerly-expected visitor had arrived. But great was my astonishment when I saw this same wild boy enter the room in quite a dignified way, and, though very lively and talkative, yet all the time preserving a certain formality. He himself impressed me even more than the account of his performances had done, and I could not help feeling a little shy during the whole of the visit.

The next day Schmitt called again, to take me to the Mendelssohns. I found the whole family assembled in a great room at the "Swan" hotel, and was very kindly received. I shall never forget the impression made on me by the mother, whom I was never to see again. She was sitting at work at a little table, and inquired about all that I was doing with an infinite kindness and gentleness that won my childish confidence at once.

There was a Frankfort quartet party in the room, but besides these I remember only young Edward Devrient, who pleased me very much, not only by his good looks and graceful ways, but also by the exquisite manner in which he sang an air of

Mozart's. We had a great deal of music : Felix played one of his quartets—in *C minor, if I recollect right ; but I was most struck by his sister Fanny's performance of Hummel's Rondeau brillant in A, which she played in a truly masterly style. Meantime I became more intimate with Felix, and at his second visit he astonished me immensely. I was showing him a violin sonata of Aloys Schmitt's, when he at once took up a violin which lay on the piano and asked me to play the sonata with him ; he got through his part very cleverly and well, though the brilliant passages were naturally somewhat sketchy.

Having thus made Mendelssohn's acquaintance, I was constantly on the watch for news of him from the many artists who came from Berlin to Frankfort, and they were never tired of singing his praises. But it was not till some years later that his abilities made a full and permanent impression on me. The " Cæcilia " Society was then in all its freshness and vigour, under the admirable direction of Schelble. Mendelssohn happened to be present at one of the practice-meetings in the spring of 1825, as he was passing through Frankfort on a holiday tour, and was asked to play. We had been singing choruses from " Judas Maccabæus." He took some of the

* Quartet for Pianoforte and Strings (Op. 2).

principal melodies—especially " See the Conquering
Hero "—and began to extemporise on them.   I
hardly know which was most wonderful—the skilful
counterpoint, the flow and continuity of the thoughts,
or the fire, expression, and extraordinary execution
which characterized his playing.   He must have been
very full of Handel at that time, for the figures
which he used were thoroughly Handelian, and the
power and clearness of his passages in thirds, sixths,
and octaves, were really grand ; and yet it all belonged to the subject-matter, with no pretension to
display, and was thoroughly true, genuine, living
music.   It quite carried me away, and though I
often heard his wonderful playing afterwards, I do
not think that it ever produced such an overpowering effect on me as it did on that occasion, when
he was but a boy of sixteen.   The next day, while
still full of what I had heard, I met another pupil
of Schmitt's, a lad of about twenty, long since dead.
We talked about Mendelssohn, and he asked me
how long I thought it would take to be able to do
all that.   I laughed.   He thought that with two
years' extra hard work it might be done.   It was
the first though by no means the last time, that
I came across anyone so foolish as to think that
genius can be got by practice.

His opinions on art and artists at that time, were
full of the vivacity natural to his age, and had in

them something—what shall I call it?—over-ripe and almost dogmatic, which as he grew up not only became balanced, but entirely disappeared. We drove over one afternoon to see André at Offenbach. On the way, I told him that it was probable I should be sent to Weimar, to continue my studies under Hummel. With this he found no fault, but I remember his speaking of Hummel very much in the condescending sort of tone in which Zelter, in his letters to Goethe, expresses himself about God and the world. And when we got to André's, I was struck with a certain precocious positiveness in his language, though all he said was full of the most genuine enthusiasm. André—one of the liveliest, brightest, and best-informed of musicians, who retained his freshness unimpaired to the end of a long life—retorted good naturedly but very sharply. André was one of those musicians who are completely wrapt up in Mozart, and who measure everything by the standard of Mozart's beauty and finish—a standard sufficient to condemn many of the finest things. Spohr's "Jessonda" and Weber's "Freischütz" were just then making their triumphant round of the theatres, and André had much to say against them. Mendelssohn, who knew by heart what the other had only a general recollection of, agreed with him in some things, and differed in others, but was most enthusiastic about the instrumentation. "How the orchestra is treated! and what a sound it has!" cried he. The tone of voice in which he uttered this kind of thing still rings in my ear; but I am convinced that such utterances were more the result of a natural endeavour to imitate his pet masters, than the real expression of his nature, which was always intensely modest. The discussion even got as far as Beethoven, whom André had often visited in Vienna. The worst thing he could find against him was his *manner* (so to speak) of composing, into which this learned theorist had had a glimpse. For instance, he told us that he had seen the manuscript of the A major Symphony, and that there were whole sheets left blank in it, the pages before and after which had no connection with each other. Beethoven had told him that these blanks would be filled up—but what continuity could there be in music so composed? Mendelssohn would not stand this, and kept on playing whole movements and bits of movements in his powerful orchestral style, till André was in such delight that he was obliged, for the moment, to stop his criticisms. Indeed, who could think of carping or cavilling after hearing Felix play the *Allegretto* of the A major Symphony?

A leaf from an album, containing a three-part canon, and dated " Ehrenbreitstein Valley, Sep-

tember 27th, 1827," gives me the clue to my next
meeting with Mendelssohn.   During the interval
I had been with Hummel at Weimar, and had made
a journey with him to Vienna, where I had published my "Opus 1," a pianoforte quartet.   I was
now again at work at home.   One day as I was
looking into the court, this time by chance, a young
man crossed it, whom I did not recognize, in a tall
shiny hat.   It turned out to be Mendelssohn, but
apparently much altered in looks.   His figure had
become broad and full, and there was a general air
of smartness about him, with none of that careless
ease which he sometimes adopted in later life.   He
was travelling with two of his fellow-students to
Horchheim, near Coblenz, with the view of spending part of the holidays at his uncle's place.   He
stayed only a short time at Frankfort, but long
enough for me to see that since our last meeting
he had grown into a man.

He was staying with Schelble; and I embrace this
opportunity to speak of that distinguished man and
musician, more especially as he was one of the first
to recognize Mendelssohn's worth, and to devote all
his influence to forwarding his music.   Schelble was
a thoroughly cultivated musician, and remarkable
as a pianist for his earnest and intelligent rendering
of classical works; his voice was a splendid baritone-
tenor, which he had cultivated in the same spirit as

his pianoforte playing, and he had formerly been on
the stage in Vienna and Frankfort. His great
musical abilities had brought him into contact with
the best artists; he had had much intercourse with
Beethoven, and was very intimate with Spohr. In
spite however of the success which his singing had
met with on the stage, he never felt at ease there—
in fact, he seems to have had no talent for acting.
Looking at his face, so fine, noble, and expressive,
but usually so serious, and his somewhat stiff bearing, one might have taken him for a scholar or a
Protestant pastor, but certainly not for an opera
singer. When, as a boy, I was first introduced to
him, he had long given up the theatre, had obtained
a first-rate position as teacher in Frankfort, and out
of small beginnings had established his most important work, the " Cæcilia " Society. Perhaps no
one ever possessed the qualities and ability necessary for conducting a choral society to so great a
degree as Schelble. A pianist and a singer, eloquent
and impressive, inspired for his work, respected by
the men, adored by the women, uniting the greatest
intelligence with the most delicate ear and the
purest taste, his influence was equally great as a
man and a musician. His oratorio performances,
as long as they were accompanied by the pianoforte
alone (the orchestra interferes too much with the
voices) were among the best that have ever taken

place. His spirit still pervades the Society; for many years it was conducted on the same principles by his pupil Messer; and at present Carl Müller is its efficient head.

Though Schelble wrote but little, he had gone very deeply into composition. His judgment, both in great and small things, was extraordinarily acute, and his remarks on music were as interesting as they were suggestive.

As he had introduced Felix into the Society when a boy, and Felix in his turn had won its enthusiastic goodwill by his marvellous gift of improvisation, so Schelble was the first, outside of Berlin, to perform Mendelssohn's choral works. Felix went to look him up directly after his arrival in Frankfort, and I accompanied him. The first things that Mendelssohn played to us were some of Moscheles' studies. They were but recently published, and Felix spoke of them with great warmth, and played several by heart with extraordinary energy and evident delight. But we wanted to hear something new of his own; and great was our astonishment when he played in the most lovely, tender, charming style, his string quartet in A minor,* which he had just completed. The impression it made on us pleased him all the more as the

---

* Quartet No. 2 (Op. 13), containing the song "Ist es wahr?"—*Ed.*

tendency of this piece had not been appreciated in his own circle, and he had a feeling of isolation in consequence. And then he played the Midsummer Night's Dream Overture! He had told me privately how long and eagerly he had been working at it—how in his spare time between the lectures at the Berlin University he had gone on extemporizing at it on the piano of a beautiful lady who lived close by. "For a whole year I hardly did anything else," he said; and certainly he had not wasted his time.

Of the failure of "Camacho's Wedding," his opera which had been produced at Berlin in the previous spring, he spoke with a mixture of fun and half-subdued vexation. He took off, for my benefit, whole dialogues between various people concerned in it, trying to give them a dramatic effect—with how much truth I do not know, but anyhow, in the most amusing and life-like manner. But I need hardly put down my own poor and uncertain recollections of these communications, since Edward Devrient, who was so closely connected with the whole thing both as a friend and an artist, has given us a detailed account of this entire episode in Mendelssohn's life.*

Felix invited me to accompany him and his

---

* "My Recollections of Felix Mendelssohn Bartholdy," &c., translated by Natalie Macfarren, page 23.

friends at least as far as Bingen, and my parents gladly gave their consent to this little excursion. At Mainz, where we stayed the night, a small boat was hired (it was still the ante-steamboat time) and stocked with all manner of eatables and drinkables, and we floated down the glorious river in great spirits. We talked, and laughed, and admired everything; and as a specimen of the sort of jokes we indulged in, I remember Mendelssohn suddenly asking one of us, "Do you know the Hebrew for snuffers?" When the "Mäusethurm" came in sight, and I said that my leave was at an end, and that I must be landed at Rüdesheim, they would not hear of my going, and I only too easily let myself be persuaded to remain. But my companions got out at Horchheim, and in the evening I found myself alone at Coblenz, in rather an uncomfortable position. The recollections of the journey home rise up so vividly before me, that my reader must kindly pardon me if I try to revive them here, more for my own satisfaction than for his.

My small store of money was very much on the decline—even in the boat I had had a vague suspicion of it—but on no account would I have borrowed from my fellow-travellers. Giving up all idea of supper I went to the post, and after I had paid for a place in the coach to Bingen, found

I had still twelve consolatory kreutzers (about 4d.).
Early in the morning I got to Bingen, and pro-
ceeded to the river-bank, which still looked quite
deserted; but the sun was rising, and it was beau-
tifully cool and still.	After a time a boatman came
up half asleep and asked whether I wanted to go
across.	"If you will put me over to Rüdesheim,"
I said, "then may Heaven reward you, for I can't
give you more than six kreutzers."	The man had
a feeling heart in his breast, and probably thought
that something was better than nothing, so he
very cheerfully took me over to the other side.
It was a glorious morning; my spirits rose, and
I began my wandering through the lovely Rheingau
with a glad heart.	My last six kreutzers I spent
in bread and pears to keep me alive; but I had
thought of a haven, into which, literally speaking,
I hoped to run, and where I trusted my wants
would be at an end.	At Bieberich, then the
capital of the Duchy of Nassau, lived the Court-
Capellmeister Rummel, whom I knew.	He was
a good-natured man, and a clever composer, who
rather abused his facility of producing; however,
he must have had his admirers, for at every
Frankfort fair his name was to be seen paraded
in the music shop of the famous Schott and Co.
How often, and how enviously, had I stood as a
boy in front of the shop, and read the many

CHAPTER II.

MENDELSSOHN'S published letters show how
variously he was affected by his visit to the
French capital—at that time also the capital
of Europe. What happened to him elsewhere,
when in contact with persons, performances, or
circumstances against which he had a prejudice,
and from which he would have preferred keeping
himself at a distance, happened here also,—
after some resistance, he was taken possession of
by them.

The few years which followed the Revolution of
July are among the best in modern French history.
The impression of the "Three days" was still fresh
in people's minds; everything had received a new
impetus, and literature and the arts especially were
full of a wonderfully stirring and exuberant life.
As to our beloved music, one could hardly wish for
a better state of things. The so-called Conservatoire
concerts, under Habeneck, were in all their fresh-

ness ; and Beethoven's Symphonies were played
there with a perfection, and received with an
enthusiasm, which, with few exceptions, I have
never since witnessed. Cherubini was writing his
Masses for the Chapel in the Tuileries ; at
the Grand Opera Meyerbeer was beginning his
series of triumphs with "Robert the Devil ;"
Rossini was writing "William Tell ;" Scribe
and Auber were at the height of their activity,
and all the best singers were collected at the
Italian Opera. Artists of all degrees of distinction
lived in Paris, or came there to win Parisian
laurels.

Baillot, though advancing in years, still played
with all the fire and poetry of youth ; Paganini
had given a series of twelve concerts at the Grand
Opera ; Kalkbrenner, with his brilliant execution,
represented the Clementi school ; Chopin had
established himself in Paris a few months before
Mendelssohn's arrival ; and Liszt, still inspired
by the tremendous impetus he had received from
Paganini, though seldom heard in public, performed the most extraordinary feats. German
chamber-music was not so much in vogue as it
afterwards became, but still Baillot's quartet-party
had its fanatical supporters, and in many German
and French houses the most serious music was
affectionately cultivated, and good players were

welcomed with delight. Under such circumstances, it may easily be imagined how warmly Mendelssohn was greeted in the best musical circles.

The first thing that I remember connected with his arrival is the "Walpurgisnacht." I still see before me the small, closely and delicately written score, as he brought it from Italy. I had it in my room for a long time, and was as delighted with it at the first reading as I have always been since. So strongly did it impress itself upon me, that the music was still perfectly familiar to me sixteen or seventeen years after, when I heard and conducted it for the first time. Another piece which he played us was the Song without Words in E (Bk. I. No. 1). He had written it in Switzerland, and evidently felt a little impatient that his friends should hear it; for immediately after his arrival he played it to Dr. Franck and myself, calling it by its newly-invented name, so often misused since. Pieces of music which one has learnt to know shortly after their composition, and which afterwards have a great popularity, are like people whom one knew as children before they became famous, and one retains through life a kind of fatherly, or at any rate godfatherly, feeling for them.

The first time I heard Mendelssohn really at

c

his best was one evening at the house of the Leo-Valentinis, in Beethoven's D major Trio. It was a peculiarity of his, that when he played new things of his own to intimate friends, he always did it with a certain reticence, which was evidently founded on a wish not to allow his playing to increase the impression made by the actual work itself. It was only in orchestral works, where his attention was fully occupied, that he allowed himself to be carried away. But in the music of the great masters he was all fire and glow. I heard him oftenest and at his best that winter, at Baillot's house, and at that of an old and much respected lady, Madame Kiéné, whose daughter, Madame Bigot (then dead), had given Felix a few music lessons when he was a boy. With Baillot he played Bach and Beethoven Sonatas, Mozart Concertos with quartet accompaniment, and splendid extempore cadenzas; also his own Piano-forte Quartet in B minor, and other things. Baillot's circle was small, but thoroughly musical and cultivated, and everything was listened to with a sort of religious devotion. Mendelssohn had brought with him to Paris the draught-score of the "Hebrides" Overture. He told me that not only was its general form and colour suggested to him by the sight of Fingal's Cave, but that the first few bars, containing the principal subject, had actually occurred to him on the spot.* The same evening he and his friend Klingemann paid a visit to a Scotch family. There was a piano in the drawing-room, but being Sunday, music was utterly out of the question, and Mendelssohn had to employ all his diplomacy to get the instrument opened for a single minute, so that he and Klingemann might hear the theme which forms the germ of that original and masterly Overture, which, however, was not completed till some years later at Düsseldorf.

Among the Parisian musicians, Habeneck took a deep interest in the gifted youth, and many of the admirable players of his orchestra were devoted to him, especially the younger ones, many of them friends of my own, whom he was always glad to see, and who clung to him with all the warm feeling of Frenchmen. Amongst them I ought especially to mention Franchomme, the excellent cello

---

* This is strictly correct. The letter to his family, describing the passage to Staffa and the inside of the cave—for the sight of which I am indebted to the kindness of Dr. Karl Mendelssohn—is dated "Auf einer Hebride, d. 7te August, 1829," as if actually written on the island. It contains the words "to show how extraordinarily moved I was, the following occurred to me"—and then come the first ten or twelve bars of the Overture in score. Six weeks after he ends a letter home, "auf Wiedersehen

F. M. B."—*Ed.*

player, and Cuvillon and Sauzay, the gifted violin
players and pupils of Baillot—the latter afterwards
his son-in-law.

"Ce bon Mendelssohn," they used to say;
"quel talent, quelle tête, quelle organisation!"
Cuvillon poured out his whole heart to him, and
Felix was quite touched in telling me of his
confidences one evening—how he had come to
Paris full of enthusiasm for Baillot, to have
lessons from him, and had fancied that such a
man must live like a prince; how he had pictured
to himself his establishment and all his way of life;
and then to find this king of violin players lodging
au troisième, in almost reduced circumstances,
giving lessons the whole day long, accompanying
young ladies on the piano, and playing in the
orchestra! It had made him quite sad, and he
could not imagine the possibility of such a state
of things.

It was through Habeneck and his "Société
des Concerts" that Mendelssohn was introduced to
the Parisian public. He played the Beethoven G
major Concerto—with what success may be seen
from his published letters.* The "Midsummer
Night's Dream Overture" was also performed and
much applauded. I was present at the first re-

* To his mother, dated Paris, 15th and 31st March, 1832.

hearsal. The second oboe was missing—which might have been overcome; but just as they were going to begin, the drummer's place was also discovered to be empty. Upon which, to everybody's amusement, Mendelssohn jumped on to the orchestra, seized the drumsticks, and beat as good a roll as any drummer in the Old Guard. For the performance a place had been given him in a box on the grand tier, with a couple of distinguished musical amateurs. During the last *forte*, after which the fairies return once more, one of these gentlemen said to the other : " C'est très-bien, très-bien, mais nous savons le reste;" and they slipped out without hearing the " reste," and without any idea that they had been sitting next the composer.

The termination of Mendelssohn's connection with that splendid orchestra was unpleasant, and hurt him much. It was proposed to give his Reformation Symphony, and a rehearsal took place. I was not present, but the only account which our young friends gave me was that the work did not please the orchestra: at any rate, it was not performed. Cuvillon's description was that it was "much too learned, too much *fugato*, too little melody," &c., &c. To a certain extent the composer probably came round to this opinion, for the Symphony was not published during his lifetime.* But at the time I am writing of he was very fond of it, and the quiet way in which it was shelved certainly pained him. I never referred to the occurrence, and he never spoke of it to me.

A few other far more painful events took place during that Paris winter. One morning Mendelssohn came into my room in tears, and at first could find no words to tell me that his friend Edward Rietz, the violinist, was dead. Everything that he said about him, the manner in which he described his ways and his playing, all showed how deeply the loss affected him. In his published correspondence, years after, I found his grief expressing itself in a higher and calmer strain, but at first it was difficult for him to control himself in the very least.

Then came the news of Goethe's death, which touched me also very deeply, though a life of such wonderful completeness should perhaps dispose one more to admiration than to regret. Mendelssohn gave me a most detailed account of his last visit to the " alter Herr," and of the sketch he had given him on the piano of the history of modern music from Bach to Beethoven. He spoke very feelingly of the terrible loss Goethe's death would

* It remained in manuscript till 1868, and was first played in England at the Crystal Palace, under the direction of Mr. Manns, on the 30th November of that year.—*Ed.*

be to old Zelter, adding : "You will see, he will not long survive it." He was right—a few months later, and Zelter followed the friend who had granted him a little corner in his palace of immortality.

On the whole, as is evident from his published letters, Mendelssohn led a pleasant easy-going life in Paris, and gave himself up to the enjoyment of the moment without hesitation. A large part of his time was devoted to chess; he was a capital player, and his usual antagonists, Michael Beer, the poet, a brother of Meyerbeer's, and Dr. Herman Franck, only occasionally succeeded in beating him. Franck would not allow that he was inferior, and upon this Mendelssohn invented a phrase which he relentlessly repeated after every victory : "We play quite equally well— *quite equally*—only I play a very little better."

Meyerbeer, who was certainly a sincere admirer of his talent, Mendelssohn saw but seldom. A funny little incident occurred shortly after his arrival in Paris. Mendelssohn was often told that he was very like the composer of "Robert;" and at first sight his figure and general appearance did perhaps give some ground for the idea, especially as they wore their hair in the same style. I sometimes teased Mendelssohn about it, to his great annoyance, and at last one morning he appeared with his hair absolutely cropt. The affair excited much amusement in our set, especially when Meyerbeer heard of it; but he took it up with his usual invincible good-nature, and in the nicest way.

Chopin had been at Munich at the same time with Mendelssohn, and had given concerts there, and otherwise exhibited his remarkable abilities. When he arrived in Paris, as a complete stranger, he met with a very kind reception from Kalkbrenner, who, indeed, deserved all praise as a most polished, clever, and agreeable host. Kalkbrenner fully recognized Chopin's talent, though in rather a patronizing way. For instance, he thought his *technique* not sufficiently developed, and advised him to attend a class which he had formed for advanced pupils. Chopin, always good-natured, was unwilling to refuse outright, and went a few times to see what it was like. When Mendelssohn heard of this he was furious, for he had a great opinion of Chopin's talent, while, on the other hand, he had been annoyed at Berlin by Kalkbrenner's charlatanry. One evening at the Mendelssohns' house there, Kalkbrenner played a grand Fantasia, and when Fanny asked him if it was an improvisation, he answered that it was. The next morning, however, they discovered the improvised Fantasia, published note for

note under the title of "Effusio musica." That
Chopin, therefore, should submit to pass for a
pupil of Kalkbrenner's seemed to Mendelssohn,
and with justice, to be a perfect absurdity, and
he freely expressed his opinion on the matter.
Meantime, the thing soon came to its natural
conclusion. Chopin gave a soirée at the Pleyel
Rooms ; all the musical celebrities were there ; he
played his E minor Concerto, some of his Mazurkas
and Notturnos, and took everybody by storm. After
this no more was heard of want of *technique,* and
Mendelssohn had applauded triumphantly.

The relations between Kalkbrenner and Mendelssohn were always somewhat insecure, but
Kalkbrenner's advances were such that Mendelssohn could not altogether decline them. We
dined there together a few times, and everything
went quite smoothly, though no entreaties could
ever persuade Felix to touch the keys of Kalkbrenner's piano. Indeed, we were none of us
very grateful for Kalkbrenner's civilities, and
took a wicked pleasure in worrying him. I remember that one day, Mendelssohn, Chopin, Liszt,
and I, had established ourselves in front of a
café on the Boulevard des Italiens, at a season
and an hour when our presence there was very
exceptional. Suddenly we saw Kalkbrenner
coming along. It was his great ambition always

to represent the perfect gentleman, and knowing how extremely disagreeable it would be to him to meet such a noisy company, we surrounded him in the friendliest manner, and assailed him with such a volley of talk that he was nearly driven to despair, which of course delighted us. Youth has no mercy.

I must here tell a little story, if indeed it deserves the name, to show what mad spirits Mendelssohn was capable of at that time. One night as we were coming home across the deserted boulevard at a late hour, in earnest conversation, Mendelssohn suddenly stops and calls out :—" We *must* do some of our jumps in Paris ! our jumps, I tell you ! Now for it ! one !— two !—three !—" I don't think my jumps were very brilliant, for I was rather taken aback by the suggestion, but I shall never forget the moment.

Soon after Mendelssohn's arrival in Paris, Dr. Franck and I were waiting for him in his room, when he came in with a beaming face and declared that he had just seen " a miracle, a real miracle ; " and in answer to our questions he continued, " Well, isn't it a miracle ? I was at Erard's with Liszt, showing him the manuscript of my Concerto,* and though it is hardly

---

* Pianoforte Concerto in G minor, Op. 25.

legible, he played it off at sight in the most
perfect manner, better than anybody else could
possibly play it—quite marvellously!" I confess
I was not so much surprised, having long known
from experience, that Liszt played most things
best the first time, because they gave him
enough to do. The second time he always had
to add something, for his own satisfaction.

I must not forget to speak of Ole Bull, the
violin player, afterwards so famous. He had
just escaped from the theological schools, and
was in Paris for the first time. His enthusiasm
for music was boundless, but of his own special
talent he gave no sign whatever. He was the
pleasantest listener imaginable, and his views
about music and musicians, expressed in very
questionable but not the less amusing German,
were a real treat to us. We often invited him
to dinner, and played to him endlessly. A few
years later, I saw him again as the celebrated
virtuoso, but the Swedish element which so
delighted me at first, had become rather a
mannerism.

Mendelssohn went occasionally to see Cherubini. "What an extraordinary creature he is!"
he said to me one day. "You would fancy
that a man could not be a great composer
without sentiment, heart, feeling, or whatever

else you call it; but I declare I believe that
Cherubini makes everything out of his head
alone." On another occasion he told me that he
had been showing him an eight-part composition,
a capella (I think it his was "Tu *es Petrus"),
and added, "The old fellow is really too pedantic:
in one place I had a suspended third in two
parts, and he wouldn't pass it on any condition."
Some years later, happening to speak of this
incident, Mendelssohn said : "The old man was
right after all; one ought not to write them."

Felix's wonderful musical memory was a
great source of enjoyment to us all as well as
to himself. It was not learning by heart, so
much as retention—and to what an extent!
When we were together, a small party of musical
people, and the conversation flagged, he would
sit down to the piano, play some out-of-the-
way piece, and make us guess the composer.
On one occasion he played an air from Haydn's
"Seasons."

> "The trav'ller stands perplexed,
> Uncertain and forlorn—"

in which not a note of the elaborate violin
accompaniment was wanting. It sounded like a
regular pianoforte piece, and we stood there

---

* Op. 111, posthumous work for voices and orchestra.

a long time as "perplexed" as the traveller himself.

The Abbé Bardin, a great musical amateur, used to get together a number of musicians and amateurs at his house once a week in the afternoons, and a great deal of music was gone through very seriously and thoroughly, even without rehearsals. I had just been playing Beethoven's E flat Concerto in public, and they asked for it again on one of these afternoons. The parts were all there, and the string quartet too, but no players for the wind. "I will do the wind," said Mendelssohn, and sitting down to a small piano which stood near the grand one, he filled in the wind parts from memory, so completely, that I don't believe even a note of the second horn was wanting, and all as simply and naturally done as if it were nothing.

It was a famous time. When we had no engagements we generally met in the afternoons. We willingly gave up lunch, so as not to have to go out in the mornings, but a little before dinner-time we used to get so frightfully hungry that a visit to the confectioner's was absolutely necessary. I believe we fasted simply to get an excuse for indulging our passion for pastry. In the evening we often went to the theatre—oftenest to the Gymnase Dramatique, for which

Scribe at that time wrote almost exclusively, and where a charming actress, Léontine Fay, had completely taken possession of us. She acted in Scribe's plays, and took the parts of young wives in doubtful situations, which call into play all their grace and sensibility. She was a slender brunette with wonderful dark eyes, an indescribable grace in her movements, and a voice that went straight to your heart. The celebrated Taglioni, the first to make that great name famous through the world, was also one of our great favourites. No one ever made me feel the poetry of dancing and pantomime as she did; it is impossible to imagine anything more beautiful and touching than her performance of the Sylphide. Börne says of her somewhere, "She flutters around herself, and is at once the butterfly and the flower," but this pretty picture conveys only a part of her charms.

I had written a pianoforte Concerto not long before, and played it in public, but the last movement did not please me, and having to play it again during this Mendelssohn winter, I determined to write a new Finale, which I secretly intended to be a picture of Léontine Fay. I had begun it, but the concert was fixed for an early day, and Mendelssohn declared I should not get my work done in time. This of course I denied,

so we made a bet of a supper upon it. My
friend's opposition excited me to make a real trial
of skill, and I scored the orchestral part of the
whole movement without putting down a note
of the solo part. The copyist too did his best,
and the result was that I contrived to play the
Concerto with the new Finale on the appointed
day. Felix paid for the supper, and Labarre, the
well-known harpist, a handsome, clever, amusing
fellow, was invited to join us. How far the portrait of Léontine Fay was successful, I leave to
be decided by its own merits, though Felix confessed that it was not unlike her.

In the midst of all these distractions, Mendelssohn seized every quiet hour for work, much
of which was a complete contrast to his actual
life at the time. It consisted generally of putting
the finishing touches to former pieces, such as
church music, his String Quintet in A, &c. Of
music absolutely new, he did not write much to
speak of during those months, but I remember
his playing me some new songs, and some short
pianoforte pieces. I had just completed my first
three Trios, and the very warm and friendly
interest which he took in them was often a
great help to me. When he liked a thing he
liked it with his whole heart, but if it did not
please him, he would sometimes use the most

singular language. One day when I had been
playing him some composition of mine, long
since destroyed, he threw himself down on the
floor and rolled about all over the room. Happily
there was a carpet! Many an evening we spent
quite quietly together talking about art and
artists over the cheerful blazing fire. On great
things we always agreed, but our views on
Italian and French composers differed consider-
ably, I being a stronger partizan for them than
he. He sometimes did not spare even the
masters whom he thought most highly of. He
once said of Handel that one might imagine
he had had his different musical drawers for
his choruses, one labelled "warlike," another
"heathen," a third "religious," and so on.

Speaking of the Opera in general he said that
he thought it had not yet produced so perfect and
complete a masterpiece as "William Tell" and
others of Schiller's dramas, but that it must be
capable of things equally great, whoever might
accomplish them. Though fully alive to the
weak points in Weber's music, he had a very
strong and almost personal affection for him.
He declared that when Weber came to Berlin
to conduct the performance of Freischütz, he
did not dare to approach him, and that once
when Weber was driving to the Mendelssohns'

house after a rehearsal, and wanted to take
Felix with him, he obstinately refused the honour,
and then ran home by a short cut at such a pace
as to be ready to open the door for the Herr
Hof-Capellmeister on his arrival.

Of all Mozart's works, I think the Zauberflöte
was the one he liked best. It seemed to him in-
expressibly wonderful that Mozart had been able
to express so exactly what he wanted, neither
more nor less, with perfect artistic consciousness,
and at once with simplest means, and the greatest
beauty and completeness.

I was unfortunately obliged to leave Paris
a few weeks before Mendelssohn, as my parents
wanted me at home. He and some other young
friends came to the well-known post-house in
the Rue J. J. Rousseau to see me off. " I really
envy you," he cried, " going off to Germany for
the spring; it's the best thing in the world ! "
After my departure, during the latter part of
his stay in Paris, he had an attack of cholera,
but, fortunately, not a severe one. From Paris
he went to London, and never returned to the
French capital.

CHAPTER III.

AIX-LA-CHAPELLE AND DÜSSELDORF—

MAY, 1834, TO MARCH, 1835.

Felix Mendelssohn to his Mother.*

DÜSSELDORF, 23*rd May*, 1834.

A WEEK ago to-day I drove to Aix-la-Chapelle
with the two Woringens; an order from the
Cabinet, five days before the festival, had
given permission for it to be held at Whitsuntide, and this order was so worded as to
render it very probable that the permission would be extended to future years. It
took us eleven hours' posting, and I was frightfully bored, and arrived cross. We went straight
to the rehearsal, and I heard a few numbers of
"Deborah," sitting in the stalls; then I told
Woringen that I must write at once to Hiller
from there, the first time for two years, because
he had done his task so admirably. Really his

---

* Vol. II. of Mendelssohn's published Letters.

work was so modest, and sounded so well, though all the time quite subordinate to Handel, and without cutting anything out; and it delighted me to find someone thinking as I do, and doing just as I should. I noticed a man with a moustache, in the front row of boxes, reading the score; and after the rehearsal, as he came down into the theatre and I went up, we met behind the scenes, and sure enough it was Ferdinand Hiller, who tumbled into my arms, ready to squeeze me to death for joy. He had come from Paris to hear the oratorio, and Chopin had cut his lessons to come with him, and so we met once more. I could now thoroughly enjoy the festival, for we three stayed together, and got a box for ourselves in the theatre where the performances took place; and the next morning of course we were all at the piano, and that was a great delight to me. They have both improved in execution, and as a pianoforte player Chopin is now one of the very first; quite a second Paganini, doing entirely new things, and all sorts of impossibilities which one never thought could be done. Hiller also is a capital player, with plenty of power, and knows how to please. They both labour a little under the Parisian love for effect and strong contrasts, and often sadly lose sight of time and calmness and real musical

feeling; perhaps I go too far the other way, so
we mutually supply our deficiencies, and all
three learn from each other, I think; meanwhile
I felt rather like a schoolmaster, and they seemed
rather like *mirliflores* or *incroyables*.   After the
festival we travelled together to Düsseldorf, and
had a very pleasant day with music and talk;
yesterday I accompanied them to Cologne, and
this morning they went up to Coblenz in the
steamer—I came down again, and the charming
episode was at an end.

In the interest of my readers I should hardly
be able to add anything to this delightful letter.
But I cannot resist the temptation of going over
this "charming episode" once more, pen in
hand, recapitulating and dwelling on it, even
where it does not especially concern the friend
to whom these pages are consecrated.

In the summer of 1833 I was living in my
mother's house in Frankfort, having lost my
father in the spring; I was then very much
taken up with Handel's Oratorios, the scores of
which had been kindly put at my disposal by
Ferdinand Ries.   "Deborah" I never saw before,
and it so pleased me that I began translating it into
German, though without any definite purpose.
I happened to tell Ries what I was doing, and

on my return to Paris with my mother in the
autumn, I received a letter from him, asking if
I felt disposed to translate the book of the
oratorio, and write additional accompaniments to
the music, for the next Lower Rhine Musical
Festival, and have it all ready by the New Year.
I accepted the proposal with the greatest delight,
got my work done by the appointed time, and
as a reward was invited to the Festival. Chopin,
with whom I was in daily and intimate intercourse, easily let himself be persuaded to go
with me, and we were busy making our
travelling plans when news arrived that the
Festival was not to take place at Whitsuntide,
though possibly later. We had hardly reconciled
ourselves to postponing our journey, when we
heard that after all permission had been granted
for Whitsuntide. I hurried to Chopin with the
news, but with a melancholy smile he answered
that it was no longer in his power to go. The
fact is that Chopin's purse was always open to
assist his emigrant Polish countrymen; he had
put aside the necessary means for the journey;
but the journey having been postponed, forty-
eight hours had been quite sufficient to empty
his cash-box. As I would not on any condition
give up his company, he said, after much consideration, that he thought he could manage it,

produced the manuscript of his lovely E flat waltz, ran off to Pleyel's with it, and came back with 500 francs! Who was happier then than I? The journey to Aix-la-Chapelle was most successful. I had the honour of being quartered in the house of the Oberbürgermeister, and Chopin got a room close by. We went straight to the rehearsal of Deborah, and there, to my great surprise and delight, I met Mendelssohn, who immediately joined us. At that time they seemed not to have much idea of his greatness at Aix-la-Chapelle, and it was only twelve years later, the year before his death, that they made up their minds to confide the direction of the Festival to him.

With the exception of some parts of Deborah, my impressions of the performances are quite effaced. But I distinctly remember the day we spent together at Düsseldorf, where the Academy, recently revived by Schadow, was then in the full vigour of youth. Mendelssohn had conducted the Festival there in the spring, and entered on his functions as musical director in the autumn. He had a couple of pretty rooms on the ground-floor of Schadow's house, was working at " St. Paul," associated a great deal with the young painters, kept a horse, and was altogether in a flourishing condition. We

spent the whole morning at his piano playing to
each other, and in the afternoon Schadow invited
us for a walk.

The general appearance and tone of the
company in which we found ourselves made an
impression on me that I shall never forget. It
was like a prophet with his disciples—Schadow,
with his noble head, his dignified easy manner, and his eloquent talk, surrounded by a
number of young men, many of them remark-
ably handsome, and the majority already great
artists, listening to him in humble silence, and
seeming to think it perfectly natural to be
lectured by him. It had become so completely
a second nature to Schadow, even outside his
studio, to act the teacher, animating and encou-
raging, or even severely lecturing, that when
Felix announced his intention of accompanying
us to Cologne on the following day, he asked
him in a serious tone what would become of
" St. Paul " with all these excursions and distractions. Mendelssohn replied quietly, but
firmly, that it would all be ready in good time.
The walk ended with coffee and a game at
bowls ; and Felix, who had been on horseback,
lent me his horse to ride home on. Chopin was
a stranger to them all, and with his usual
extreme reserve had kept close to me during the

walk, watching everything, but making his observations to me alone in the softest of voices. Schadow, always hospitable, asked us to come again in the evening, and we then found some of the most rising young painters there. The conversation soon became very animated, and all would have been right if poor Chopin had not sat so silent and so little noticed. However, Mendelssohn and I knew that he would have his revenge, and were secretly rejoicing at the thought. At last the piano was opened; I began, Mendelssohn followed; then we asked Chopin to play, and rather doubtful looks were cast at him and us. But he had hardly played a few bars, before everybody in the room, especially Schadow, was transfixed; nothing like it had ever been heard. They were all in the greatest delight, and begged for more and more. Count Almaviva had dropped his disguise, and everyone was dumb.

The next day Felix accompanied us on the steamer to Cologne. We arrived late in the afternoon, and he took us to see the Apostles' Church, and to the Bridge, where we parted in rather a comic way. I was looking down into the river, making some extravagant remark or other, when Mendelssohn suddenly calls out : "Hiller getting sentimental; heaven help us! Adieu, farewell"—and was gone.

A year afterwards I received the following
letter :—

DÜSSELDORF, *February* 26*th*, 1835.

DEAR HILLER,—I want to ask you a favour.
No doubt you will think it very wrong of me to
begin my first letter in this way, and not to have
written to you long since of my own accord. I
think so too ; but when you consider that I am
the worst correspondent in the world, and also
the most overworked man (Louis Philippe perhaps
excepted), you will surely excuse me. So pray
listen to the following request, and think of
happier times, and then you will fulfil it.

You will remember from last year how the
second day at the Musical Festivals is generally
arranged. A Symphony, an Overture, and two
or three large pieces for chorus and orchestra,
something of the style and length of Mozart's
"Davidde penitente ;" or even shorter and more
lively, or with quite secular words, or only one
long piece—such as Beethoven's "Meerestille," for
instance. I am about to conduct the Cologne
Festival this time, and I want to know whether
Cherubini has written anything that would do
for the second day's performance, and whether,
if in manuscript, he would let me have it.
You told me that you were on very good terms

with him, and I am sure you can get me the
best information on the point. If printed, pray
say what you think of it, and give me the full
title, that I may send for it. The words may
be Latin, Italian, or French, and the contents,
as I said before, sacred or otherwise. The chief
condition is that it should employ both chorus
and orchestra; and if it were a piece of some
length, say half-an-hour, I should like it to be
in several movements; or, if there is no long
piece, I should even like a single short one. It
appears that he wrote a number of grand
Hymns for the Revolution, which ought to be
very fine; might not one of these do? It is
impossible to see anything of the kind here,
and it would only take you a couple of hours
or a walk or two; so I am convinced you can
do what I ask, especially as you are intimate
with Cherubini, and he will therefore tell you
directly what he has written in this line, and
where it is to be found.

It would of course be best if we could find
something quite unknown to musicians. You
may imagine how glad the whole committee,
and all the company of Oberbürgermeisters,
and the entire town of Cologne, and all the rest,
would be to write to Cherubini and make this
application. And of course they would also

willingly be charged something for it; but, with his strange ways, they might catch him in an evil hour, and probably he does not care much about it : therefore it is better for you to undertake the matter, and write to me what is to be done next. All that I want is to have nothing but really fine music on the second day, and that is why this request is important to me, and why I count on your fulfilling it.

Then I shall at the same time hear how life goes with you on your railway. Sometimes I hear about it through the *Messager* or the *Constitutionnel*, when you give a Soirée, or play Bach's Sonatas with Baillot; but it is always very short and fragmentary. I want to know if you have any regular and continuous occupation, whether you have been composing much, and what, and if you are coming back to Germany. So you see I am the same as ever.

My Oratorio* will be quite ready in a few weeks, and I hear from Schelble that it is to be performed by the Cæcilia Society in October; I have some new pianoforte things, and shall shortly publish some of them. I always think of you and your warning whenever an old-fashioned passage comes into my head, and

---

* St. Paul, first performed at Düsseldorf at the Lower Rhine Festival, May 22, 1836.—*Ed.*

hope to get rid of such ideas. You will of course conclude from this that I often think of you, but you might believe that anyhow. My three Overtures are not out yet; Härtel writes to me to-day that they are at the binder's, and will be here in a few days. I shall send you a copy as I promised at the first opportunity, and as soon as my new Symphony comes out, you shall have that too. I will gladly release you from your promise of sending me those plaster caricatures in return, and ask you instead to let me have some copies of new compositions, which I should like a great deal better. Remember me to Chopinetto, and let me know what new things he has been doing; tell him that the military band here serenaded me on my birthday, and that amongst other things they played his B flat Mazurka with trombones and big drum; the passage in G flat with two bass bassoons was enough to kill one with laughing. *A propos*, the other day I saw Berlioz's Symphony, arranged by Liszt, and played it through, and once more could not imagine how you can see anything in it. I cannot conceive anything more insipid, wearisome, and Philistine, for with all his endeavours to go stark mad, he never once succeeds; and as to your Liszt with his two fingers on one key, what does a homely provincial like me want with him ? What is the good of it all ? But still it must be nicer in Paris than here, if it were only for Frau von S. (Frau von M.'s sister), who is really too pretty, and is now in Paris (here there's not a soul that's pretty). And then there's plenty of agreeable society (remember me to Cuvillon, Sauzay, and Liszt, also to Baillot a thousand times ; but not to Herr —— nor Madame —— nor the child ; and tell Chopin to remember me to Eichthal), and it's always so amusing there,—but still I wish you would come to Germany again.

I have gossipped long enough. Mind you answer very soon, as soon as you can tell me what I want to know, and remember me to your mother, and keep well and happy.

Your

FELIX MENDELSSOHN BARTHOLDY.

DÜSSELDORF, *March* 14, 1835.

DEAR HILLER,—Many thanks for your dear kind letter, which gave me very great pleasure. It's not right of you to say that I should be forced on account of the business to write to you again, because I should have done so at any rate ; and if you want to try, you had

better answer at once, and then you will see
how soon I shall write again. I should so like
to know all about your life, and what you do,
and be able to picture it to myself thoroughly.

About my own I have not much to say, but
there is no thought of my leaving Germany and
going to England; who can have told you such
a thing? Whether I stay at Düsseldorf longer
than I am bound by my contract, which comes
to an end next October, is another question; for
there is simply nothing to be done here in the
way of music, and I long for a better orchestra,
and shall probably accept another offer that I
have had. I wanted to be quite free for a few
years, and go on a sort of art-journey, and snap
my fingers at musical directorships and the like;
but my father does not wish it, and in this I
follow him unconditionally. You know that
from the very beginning all I wanted here was a
really quiet time for writing some larger works,
which will be finished by October; and so I
hope to have made use of my stay. Besides it
is very pleasant, for the painters are capital
fellows, and lead a jolly life; and there is
plenty of taste and feeling for music; only the
means are so limited that it is unprofitable in
the long run, and all one's trouble goes for
nothing. I assure you that at the beat, they all

come in separately, not one with any decision, and in the *pianos* the flute is always too high, and not a single Düsseldorfer can play a triplet clearly, but all play a quaver and two semi-quavers instead, and every *Allegro* leaves off twice as fast as it began, and the oboe plays E natural in C minor, and they carry their fiddles under their coats when it rains, and when it is fine they don't cover them at all—and if you once heard me conduct this orchestra, not even four horses could bring you there a second time. And yet there are one or two musicians among them, who would do credit to any orchestra, even to your Conservatoire; but that is just the misery in Germany—the bass trombones and the drum and the double bass excellent, and everything else quite abominable. There is also a choral society of 120 members, which I have to coach once a week, and they sing Handel very well and correctly, and in the winter there are six subscription concerts, and in the summer every month a couple of masses, and all the *dilettanti* fight to the death, and nobody will sing the solos, or rather everybody wants to, and they hate putting themselves forward, though they are always doing it; but you know what music is in a small German town—Heaven help us!

This is certainly rather an odd way of coming back to the question of your returning to Germany. But still the very agreeable and telling way in which you refused my dinner-invitation does not yet repel me. On the contrary, I should like you for once to answer the question seriously : Is there any condition on which you would like to live in Germany? and if so, what? In the theoretical way we talked of it in front of the Post-house at Aix-la-Chapelle, we shall never get far in the matter. But now I should like to know whether, if for instance a place like Hummel's, or like Spohr's at Cassel, or Grund's at Meiningen, in short any Capellmeister's place at one of the ˋsmall courts were vacant, you would accept such a thing, and make up your mind to leave Paris? Would the pecuniary advantages be of any great importance to you? or are you not thinking of coming back in any case? or are you too much tied by the attractions and excitements of your present life? Pray don't be vexed with me for all these questions, and answer them as fully as you can. It is always possible that some place may turn up in Germany, and you can imagine how I should like to have you nearer, both for my own sake and the sake of good music.

And now to business; and first I must thank you very much for the prompt and satisfactory way in which you have managed the thing for us. I should like best if you would send me the Motet in E flat, "Iste die," with the "Tantum ergo" for five voices, and at the same time *also* the Coronation March from the Mass *du Sacre.* That is what I want.

A Herr Bel from Cologne will call on you, and ask for these things. Please let him have them to send to me, and tell him what you have spent, and he will reimburse you—and again many thanks to you. I have not yet received your studies and songs from Frankfort, but on the other hand the *Rêveries* are lying on my piano, because an acquaintance of mine gets the French paper and always sends it to me whenever there is anything of yours or Chopin's in it. The one in F sharp major is my favourite and pleases me very much, and the A flat one is quaint and charming. But do tell me exactly what you have been doing and are going to do. I see from what you say that you are proposing some great work, but you don't tell me what it is. . . . .

Yours, F. M. B.

P.S. Bendemann, Schirmer, and Hildebrand all

E

beg to be remembered to you, and hope that you will soon be here again.

At the end of 1847, when I came to Düsseldorf as Director, I found the music there on quite a different footing from that which Mendelssohn had described. The twelve years' energy which Julius Rietz had devoted to it had not been in vain. On my removal to Cologne in 1850, I managed to secure the post for Robert Schumann.

CHAPTER IV.

My dear mother had given up living in Paris, so as to leave me free for a journey to Italy, which I had long wished to undertake. We returned to Frankfort in the spring of 1836, and immediately after our arrival I hurried off to Düsseldorf. The Lower Rhine Musical Festival was to take place there that year under Mendelssohn's direction, and "St. Paul" was to be performed for the first time. The concert was held at the Becker-garden (now the so-called "Rittersaal" belonging to the town music-hall), but the room was too small for the large audience and orchestra, and in the "Sleepers wake" chorus, the blast of the trumpets and trombones from the gallery down into the low hall was quite overpowering. I had arrived too late for rehearsal, and, sitting there all alone, listening to an entirely new work, in a frightfully hot and close room, was naturally not so deeply impressed as I expected to be. But the audience, who had already heard it three or four times, were delighted; the performers were thoroughly inspired; and on the third day, when, among other things, the chorus "Rise up, arise" was repeated, I listened with very different ears, and was as enthusiastic as anybody. The oratorio afterwards grew on me more and more, especially the first part, which I now consider one of the noblest and finest of Mendelssohn's works.

Mendelssohn was in every way the centre-point of the Festival, not only as composer, director, and pianist, but also as a lively and agreeable host, introducing the visitors to each other, and bringing the right people together, with a kind word for everybody. There I saw Sterndale Bennett for the first time, renewed my boyish friendship with Ferdinand David, and greatly enjoyed meeting the young painters of Schadow's school, many of them already famous. The only musical part of the Festival which I remember, besides "St. Paul," was the marvellously spirited and perfect performance of the Kreutzer Sonata by Mendelssohn and David on the third day.

A few days after my return, Felix followed me to Frankfort. The first thing which he encountered there was a report of the Festival (the only one he had seen), in which "St. Paul" was spoken of in that lofty, patronizing, damaging tone too often adopted by critics towards artists who stand high above them. It was some time before he could get over the fact that the first criticism of his beloved work should be so offensive—thus the writer had gained his object.

Our excellent friend Schelble had been obliged by illness to retire to his home at Hüfingen near Baden, and during his absence Mendelssohn had promised to undertake the direction of the "Cæcilia" Society for him. He took it only for six weeks, but during that short time his influence was most inspiring. He made them sing Handel and Bach, especially the wonderfully beautiful cantata by the latter, "Gottes Zeit ist die allerbeste Zeit." He had the art of communicating his own enthusiasm to the chorus, so as completely to electrify them. At the same time he won all hearts by his invariable good-nature and kindness in every act and word.

Mendelssohn was living in a large house belonging to Schelble, which stood at the corner of the "Schöne Aussicht," with a splendid view up and down the river, and was very comfortable there. He enjoyed receiving his friends, and even loved an occasional interruption from sympathetic visitors in the morning. Our house, at the "Pfarreisen," was not far off, and we saw a great deal of each other. My dear mother, who in spite of her intense love for me could easily be enthusiastic about talents which surpassed my own, was in raptures with Mendelssohn, and ready to do anything for him that lay in her power. She soon discovered his favourite dishes and knew how to indulge him in so many little ways, that he felt quite at home with us. She would often secretly order a carriage for us, so that we might make excursions in the beautiful environs of Frankfort. On one of these expeditions I had the opportunity of seeing my friend in rather a passion. It was near the village of Bergen. The coachman did or said some stupidity or other, upon which Mendelssohn jumped out of the carriage in a towering rage, and after pouring a torrent of abuse upon the man, declared that nothing should make him get in again. The punishment was on our side, and my mother was quite frightened when we arrived late in the evening, hot and exhausted, having had to walk the whole way home. At supper Felix himself could not help laughing, though still stoutly maintaining that he was right.

I remember that one day, after dinner, Men-

delssohn found my Studies lying on the piano,
and instantly sat down and played off the whole
four-and-twenty one after the other in the most
splendid style.   My mother was in ecstasy.   "He
is a wonderful man, that Felix," she said to me,
beaming with delight.   He, meanwhile, was in
the greatest spirits at having given us pleasure,
but so hot and excited that he went off at once
to my room, to the leathern sofa on which he
was so fond of rolling about.

We had many pleasant and interesting visitors
at that time, amongst others the famous Swedish
song-writer Lindblad, whose northern accent
added a peculiar charm to his liveliness and
gaiety.   His visit was short, but we saw a
great deal of him.   One morning, after Mendelssohn had played his Overture to Melusine,
he said, "That music listens to itself!"   Perhaps
it does—and it must be delighted with what it
hears.

A special interest was given to that spring
by Rossini's visit to Frankfort, and his almost
daily meetings with Mendelssohn at our house.
This most renowned of all Maestros had come
to Frankfort with the Baroness James Rothschild, for the wedding of one of the younger
members of the family—in the Baroness's mind
no doubt to add to the glory of the feast by

his presence. She was a highly cultivated lady, and knew Rossini's best points, having had plenty of opportunity, during their long journey, of observing his deep appreciation of whatever was beautiful, and his delight in art and nature. Since his "William Tell," Rossini had reached the highest pinnacle of his fame, and was now also at the height of his personality, if I may so express myself. He had lost the enormous corpulence of former years : his figure was still full, but not disproportioned, and his splendid countenance, which displayed both the power of the thinker and the wit of the humourist, beamed with health and happiness. He spoke French quite as well as Italian, and with the most melodious voice : his long residence in Paris, and intercourse with the best people there, had transformed him from a haughty young Italian into a man of the world, dignified, graceful, and charming, and enchanting everybody by his irresistible amiability. He had come to see us one morning, to our great delight, and was describing his journey through Belgium, and all that had struck him there, when I heard the bell, and feeling certain that it was Mendelssohn, ran out to open the door of the corridor. It was Felix, and with him Julius Rietz, who had just arrived. I told them that Rossini was there, and Mendelssohn was delighted; but, in spite of all our persuasions, Rietz would not come in, and turned back. When Felix appeared, Rossini received him with marked respect, and yet in such a friendly manner, that in a few minutes the conversation resumed its flow and became quite animated. He wanted Mendelssohn to play to him, and after a little resistance on Mendelssohn's side, they arranged to meet at our house again next morning. These meetings were often repeated in the course of the next few days, and it was quite charming to see how Felix, though inwardly resisting, was each time afresh obliged to yield to the overwhelming amiability of the Maestro, as he stood at the piano listening with the utmost interest, and expressing his satisfaction more or less openly. I cannot deny the fact—and indeed it was perfectly natural — but Felix, with his juvenile looks, playing his compositions to a composer whose melodies just then ruled the whole world of song, was, in a certain measure, ostensibly acting an inferior part—as must always be the case when one artist introduces himself to another without any corresponding return. Mendelssohn soon began to rebel a little. "If your Rossini," said he to me one morning when we met at our bath in the Main, "goes on mutter-

ing such things as he did yesterday, I won't
play him anything more."

"What did he mutter? I did not hear
anything."

"But I did: when I was playing my F
sharp minor Caprice, he muttered between his
teeth, ' *Ça sent la sonate de Scarlatti.*' "

"Well, that's nothing so very dreadful."

"Ah—bah!"

However, on the following day he played to
him again. I must add that Rossini always
looked back to this meeting with Mendelssohn
with heartfelt pleasure, and expressed the
strongest admiration for his talent.

The impression made by Rossini on the
whole colony of Frankfort musicians was really
overwhelming. The second day after his arrival
I had to drive about with him to all the artists
of importance, and with many of them to act
the part of interpreter. Some were ready to
faint with fear and surprise when he appeared.
My mother afterwards invited all these gentlemen,
and one or two foreign artists who happened
to be staying in Frankfort, to meet him at a
soirée; and it was almost comic to see how
each did his best to shine before the great
leader of the light Italian school. Capellmeister
Guhr played a sonata of his own, Ferdinand

Ries the Study with which he had first made a sensation in London, Aloys Schmitt a Rondo, and some one else a Notturno. Mendelssohn was intensely amused at the whole thing. Rossini was more pompous that evening than I ever remember to have seen him; very polite, very amiable, and very complimentary—in fact, *too* complimentary. But next day his sly humour came out. A grand dinner had been arranged in his honour at the "Mainlust," and as many celebrities of all kinds as there were room for took part in it, Mendelssohn among the rest. When the dinner was over, the hero of the day began walking up and down the garden and talking in his usual way; meanwhile the place had become crowded with people who wanted to see the great man, and who pushed and squeezed and peered about to get a peep at him, he all the time pretending to ignore them utterly. I have never witnessed such a personal ovation to a composer in the open air—except, perhaps, on his way to the grave!

The year 1836 was one of the most important of Mendelssohn's life, for it was that in which he first met his future wife. Madame Jeanrenaud was the widow of a clergyman of the French Reformed Church in Frankfort. Her

husband had died in the prime of life, and she
was living with her children at the house of her
parents, the Souchays, people of much distinction in the town. Felix had been introduced
to them, and soon felt himself irresistibly
attracted by the beauty and grace of the eldest
daughter, Cécile. His visits became more and
more frequent, but he always behaved with such
reserve towards his chosen one, that, as she
once laughingly told me in her husband's presence, for several weeks she did not imagine
herself to be the cause of Mendelssohn's visits,
but thought he came for the sake of her
mother, who, indeed, with her youthful vivacity,
cleverness, and refinement, chattering away in
the purest Frankfort dialect, was extremely
attractive. But though during this early time
Felix spoke but little to Cécile, when away
from her he talked of her all the more. Lying
on the sofa in my room after dinner, or taking
long walks in the mild summer nights with
Dr. S. and myself, he would rave about her
charm, her grace, and her beauty. There was
nothing overstrained in him, either in his life
or in his art : he would pour out his heart
about her in the most charmingly frank and
artless way, often full of fun and gaiety ; then
again, with deep feeling, but never with any

exaggerated sentimentality or uncontrolled passion. It was easy to see what a serious thing it was, for one could hardly get him to talk of anything which did not touch in some way upon her. At that time I did not know Cécile, and therefore could only act the sympathetic listener. How thankless the part of confidant is, we learn from French tragedies; and I had not even the satisfaction of being sole confidant, for S. was often present during Felix's outpourings; but on the other hand he and I could talk over all these revelations, and our affection for Mendelssohn made it easy for us to forgive the monotony which must always pervade a lover's confidences. Mendelssohn's courtship was no secret, and was watched with much curiosity and interest by the whole of Frankfort society; and many remarks which I heard showed me that to possess genius, culture, fame, amiability, and fortune, and belong to a family of much consideration as well as celebrity, is in certain circles· hardly enough to entitle a man to raise his eyes to a girl of patrician birth. But I do not think that anything of this sort ever came to Mendelssohn's ears.

In the beginning of August he went to the seaside for the benefit of his health, and also, as Devrient tells us on good authority, to test his

love by absence. Soon after he left, I received
the following letter from the Hague; and his
humorous irritation shows even more plainly
than his pathetic complaints, how hard he found
it to bear the few weeks' separation.

'S GRAVENHAGE, *7th August,* 1836.

DEAR HILLER,—How I wish I were at the
Pfarreisen with you, telling you about Holland,
instead of writing to you about it. I think it
is impossible in Frankfort to have any idea of
how dull it is at the Hague.

If you don't answer this letter directly,
and write me at least eight pages about Frankfort and the Fahrthor,* and about yourself and
your belongings, and music, and all the living
world, I shall probably turn cheesemonger here
and never come back again. Not one sensible
thought has come into my head since I drove
out of the Hôtel de Russie; I am now beginning
by degrees to accustom myself to it a little, and
have given up hoping for any sensible ideas,
and only count the days till I go back, and
rejoice that I have already taken my sixth bath
to-day, about a quarter of the whole penalty. If
you were me, you would already have packed up

---

* The Jeanrenauds lived close to the " Fahrthor."

ten times, turned your back on the cheese-
country, said a few incomprehensible words to
your travelling companion, and gone home again;
I should be glad enough to do so, but a certain
Philistinism that I am known to possess holds
me back. I had to stay three days instead of
two at Düsseldorf, because it was impossible to
get S. away, and I think those few days did
a good deal towards making me melancholy.
There was such an air of the past about everything, and fatal remembrance—for which you
know I care but little—would play its part
again. The ·Festival is said to have been fine,
but that did not make the time less tedious.
I had to hear no end about Schindler and his
writings and refutations, and it was not amusing.
I dined at ——, and that also recalled bygone
times.

Rietz is for the moment recovered, but looks
so dreadfully ill and worried, and is so overworked by the musical set at Düsseldorf, and
so ill-treated by others, that it made my heart
ache to see him. We had rain on the steamer
as far as Rotterdam; Schirmer came on here
with us, and then went by steamer to Havre,
and after that to Paris—but oh! I wish I were
at the Pfarreisen!—for all the real bother
began here. S. got cross, and found everything

too dear, and we couldn't get a lodging or a
carriage, and the Dutch did not understand
German, though S. boldly addressed them all
in it; and his boy was naughty, and there was
no end of bother. We have got a lodging at
the Hague now, and drive out to Scheveningen
every morning at eight, and take our bath, and
are all in good working order. However, nothing
can destroy the effect of the sea out at Scheveningen, and the straight green line is as mysterious
and unfathomable as ever, and the fish and shells
which the tide washes up on the shore are pretty
enough. But still the sea here is as prosaic
as it can possibly be anywhere; the sand-hills
look dreary and hopeless, and one sees hardly
any reflection in the water, because the level of
the coast is so low; half the sea is just the
colour of the shore, because it is very shallow
at first, and only begins to be deep far out.
There are no big ships, only middling-sized
fishing-boats; so I don't feel cheerful, though a
Dutchman caught hold of me to-day as I was
running along the shore and said, " Hier solle se
nu majestuosische Idee sammele." I thought to
myself, "It's a pity you are not in the land
where the pepper grows and I in the wine-
country." One can't even be really alone, for
here too there are musical people, and they take

offence if you snub them. There are actually
some Leipsic ladies, who bathe at Scheveningen
and go about afterwards with their hair all down
their backs, which looks disgusting, and yet
you're expected to pay them attention. My only
consolation is Herr von ——, which shows how
far gone I am; but he also is bored to death,
and that is why we harmonize. He keeps looking
at the sea as if he could have it tapped to-
morrow if he chose; but that does not matter,
and I like walking with him better than with
the Leipsic ladies and their long hair. Lastly, I
have to teach S.'s boy, help him with his Latin
construing from Cornelius Nepos, mend his pens,
cut his bread and butter, and make tea for
him every morning and evening, and to-day I
had to coax him into the water, because he
always screamed so with his father and was so
frightened—and this is how I live at the Hague,
and I wish I were at the Pfarreisen.

But do write soon and tell me all about it,
and comfort me a little. . . . That was a good
time we had in Frankfort, and as I seldom talk
about such things, I must tell you now how heartily
thankful I am to you for it. Those walks at
night by the Main, and many an hour at your
house, and the afternoons when I lay on your
sofa, and you were so frightfully bored and I

F

not at all—I shall never forget them. It really is a great pity that we meet so seldom and for such short times; it would be such a pleasure to us both if it could be otherwise. Or perhaps you think we should quarrel at last? I don't believe it.*

Have you ever, since I went away, thought of our Leipsic overture which I am so fond of? Do let me find it finished when I come back; it will only take you a couple of afternoons now, and hardly anything but copying. And my pianoforte piece, how about that? I have not thought of music here yet, but I have been drawing and painting a good deal, and I may also perhaps bring back some music. What is the Cæcilia Society doing? Is it alive still, or sleeping and snoring? Many things belonging to our Frankfort time are over . . . X. told me to-day that H. is engaged to be married : is it true? Then you also must marry soon. I propose Madame M. Have you seen her again, and the Darmstadt lady? Write to me about all Frankfort. Tell Mdlle. J. that there is only one engraving hanging in my room here, but it represents *la ville de Toulon*, and so I always have to think of her as a

---

* See page 216.—*Ed.*

Toulonese. And mind you remember me to your mother most particularly, and write to me very very soon. If my patience is not exhausted, I shall stay here till the 24th or 26th of August, and then travel by land or water back to the Free-town of Frankfort. Oh that I were there now! If you show this letter to anybody I wish you may be roasted, and anyhow I should be hanged; so lock it up or burn it, but write to me at once, *poste restante, à la Haye.* Farewell, and think nicely of me and write soon.

Your F. M. B.

It will easily be conceived that I did not burn this letter, and I shall hardly be blamed for not keeping it locked up any longer. A few days after I received it I met with a little accident. Jumping into the swimming-bath in a shallow part of the river, I trod on a sharp piece of glass, and must have cut a small vein, for when, with a good deal of pain, I got to land, a little fountain of blood sprang from the wound. I was more amused than frightened at the sight, but towards evening a kind of nervous attack came on, which made me feel very weak and ill. A few days later the doctor recommended change of air, and sent me to

Homburg, at that time a most retired and idyllic little spot. There was one small house near the mineral spring, in which my mother and I established ourselves : the whole bathing-population consisted only of some two dozen Frankforters. From Homburg I sent Mendelssohn a report of myself, and received the following answer :—

THE HAGUE, 18*th August*, 1836.

DEAR FERDINAND,—This is very bad news which your letter gives me, and the whole tone of it is so low-spirited that it shows what a tiresome and serious illness you have gone through. I hope you are getting on better, and that these lines will find you in quite a different frame of mind from the one you wrote in ; but as you had to be sent to the country, the thing must have been rather obstinate, and if with your strong constitution you had nervous attacks, and suffered from exhaustion, it must really have been serious, and you must have needed much patience, poor fellow ! I only hope that it is all over now, and that I shall find you in Frankfort again quite strong and well. It is curious that I also should have hurt my foot bathing, about a week or ten days ago

(much less seriously than you, of course, only
sprained), and since that time I limp about
laboriously, which certainly creates a sort of
sympathy between us, though it only makes the
stay here more tiresome ; for if one can't give full
play to one's body (in a twofold sense) in a
bathing-place like this, one really has nothing
else to do. In fact, if you expect this to be a
cheerful letter I am afraid you must take the
will for the deed, for I am much too full of
whims now that I have to limp about, and am
no good as a comforter. Besides this, S. took
himself off a few days ago, and has left me here
alone amongst the people "who speak a strange
tongue." So now I have to swallow all the
ennui by myself—we used at least to be able
to swear in company. The bathing seemed to
exhaust him too much, and he was afraid
of getting seriously ill, so I could hardly press
him to stay, and he is probably already
sitting comfortably and quietly at Düsseldorf,
whilst I have our whole apartment to myself,
and can sleep in three beds if I like. Twenty-
one baths make up what they call the small
cure, the minimum that can do one any good,
and when these are finished I shall be off
in a couple of hours, and I look forward to
Emmerich and the Prussian frontier as if it

were Naples or something equally beautiful.
Next Monday I shall take this long-expected
twenty-first bath, and my plan is to go up the
Rhine by steamer, as unfortunately there is no
quicker way. I must stop a day at Horchheim,
at my uncle's, for on the way here I hardly
stopped at all; and I hope to goodness on
Sunday evening, the 28th August, I may celebrate Goethe's birthday at Frankfort in Rhine
wine; and as I write this you can't imagine
how I long for the time. Shall we be able to
spend the evening together directly? I am
always afraid you will stay too long at your
Homburg, and who knows whether I should be
able to go and see you there? Whereabouts is
this Homburg? Is it Homburg vor der Höhe, or
Hessen-Homburg where the Prince comes from,
or which? Just now it seems to me as if I
had also heard of one in the Taunus; if so,
and that be yours, could not we meet somewhere between Frankfort and Mainz on the
28th? That would be splendid, and we would
come along together past the watch-tower into
Frankfort, and have such a fine talk all the
evening. Please write me a few lines about
it, and about how you are—you would be
doing me a great kindness; only say how and
when I am to meet you, and give me good

news of yourself and your belongings. I can plainly see from your letter that it was an effort to you, and I thank you all the more for having written it, but you must please make another good effort, even if it is only a few lines, and address it to Herrn Mendelssohn, Coblenz, and then I shall get it quick and sure. I am drawing a great deal, but composing little; but I wish I were at the Pfarreisen. Forgive this stupid letter; farewell, and may we have a happy meeting on the Main, in good health.

Always your F. M. B.

In consequence of this letter I must have offered to meet Mendelssohn at Höchst, which I could easily reach from Homburg. Nothing came of it, however, as may be seen from the following note :—

COBLENZ, 27*th August*, 1836.

DEAR OLD DRAMA,*—I got your letter yesterday at Cologne, and can only answer it

---

* I had given my first Concert Overture in D minor, which I have mentioned once or twice, the title of "Overture to the Old Drama of Fernando;" this brought about the expressions "Old Drama," and the like, which we shall find often repeated. When it was published I omitted the title, as it referred to a drama which is only now by degrees becoming an old one.

to-day from here in great haste, for it is better to talk than write. I shall not be able to say exactly when I go from Mainz to Frankfort, and come to Höchst. I have to have leeches on my stupid foot to-day, *par ordre de moufti (chirurgien),* and so must stay here to-morrow, and keep quiet; it would be too horrible to come to Frankfort and have to stay in. I hope to be able to come on Monday evening, but I may still perhaps start to-morrow morning, and in any case I am too uncertain to be able to give you a *rendezvous.* I must obey the leeches; but anyhow I could not have gone to Homburg with you; I feel myself far too much drawn to the old Free-town, and you know how I long to be there. Do come back there soon, and let me find a line from you, *poste restante,* Frankfort, to say how and when you will come, so that I may meet you. Remember me to your people, and keep well and happy, in major, and 6-4 chords of all sorts.

Your F. M. B.

Mendelssohn's engagement took place during my stay at Homburg—a great event, and much spoken of. He called on us one afternoon with his *fiancée* and her sister, but as he had only

a very short time to be with her, one could
not make any demands on so happy a lover.
Towards the end of September, if not sooner, he
was obliged to return to his Leipsic duties, and
could not even remain for a great rural festivity*
given at the " Sandhof" by the grandparents of
Cécile, to celebrate the engagement.   He went
off, with post-horses, in an old carriage which
my mother lent him.   I had put off my journey
to Italy, so as to undertake the direction of the
Cæcilia Society, and shortly afterwards received
the following letter:—

LEIPSIC, 29*th October*, 1836.

MY DEAR FERDINAND,—Cécile says you are
angry with me, but I say, don't be so, at least,
not very, for my long silence really may be
forgiven.   You cannot have any idea of the heap
of work that is put upon me; they really push
it too far with music here, and the people never
can get enough.   I have rehearsals almost every
day, sometimes two, or rehearsal and concert
the same day, and when I am tired and done
up with talking and beating time, I don't like
then to sit down and write to you.   If you

---

* See published letter, July 3, 1839; and also page 187.—*Ed.*

had been a really nice fellow you would long
ago have sent me a few lines, and have thought,
" As he does not write first, he probably can't,
so I will," and certainly you are not as driven
and worried as I am. And then you often see
Cécile, and you might have written to me about
her, and you don't do it a bit, and yet you
expect to be called generous ! But I won't
complain if you will make up for it directly,
and write and describe everything that has
happened to you since the 19th of September
at midnight.

About myself there is really nothing to say.
I conduct the Subscription Concerts and divers
others, and I wish with all my heart I were at
the Fahrthor. You have plenty to write
about — how you are living, how your people
are, whether you have time and inclination for
composing, how my pianoforte piece is getting
on, and the Cæcilia Society ; how my bride is
looking, how you get on in their house ; about
Schelble, about the fat P., about all Frankfort
(where I would so gladly be, and you perhaps in
Leipsic), all this you must write about, and
do it very soon, dear Ferdinand.

After all I have something to tell you about,
and that is our second Subscription Concert and
your Overture in E, with which you gave me

and all of us such real and heartfelt pleasure.
It sounded extremely fresh and beautiful with the
orchestra, and was played with real liking; some
parts, from which on the piano I had not
expected so much, came out admirably in the
orchestra, especially one where it goes down
fortissimo in semibreves (your favourite passage,
very broad and strong) and sounds splendid,
and my wind instruments went at it so heartily
that it was quite a treat. David made the
strings do it all with the down bow—you should
have heard it; and then the softness of the wind
instruments, and the return to E major *pianis-
simo!* The whole composition gave me more
pleasure than ever, and I liked it better than
any of the new things that I know. The so-called
public were less delighted than I had expected
and wished, because it is just the kind of thing
that they can and ought to understand; but I
think it comes from their not yet having
seen your name to any orchestral composition,
which always makes them chary of their enthusiasm in Germany. So it's lucky that the
Director of the theatre sent the very next day
to ask for the Overture for a concert which is to
be given in the theatre in a week or two, and I
promised it him. (I hope you don't mind.) On
the 8th of January we do the one in D minor,

and towards the end of the winter I shall
probably repeat both. I don't know what the
reviews have said about it, for I did not read
them; Fink said to me that it was "beautiful
writing," and Sch . . was going to write at length
about it—God grant it may be something good.*
But what does it matter? The generality of
musicians here were very much pleased with it,
and that is the chief thing. But when is my
pianoforte piece coming?

You had better not boast so much about your
Cæcilia Society; we Leipzigers are getting up a
performance of "Israel in Egypt," which will
be something quite perfect; more than 200
singers, with orchestra and organ, in the church;
I look forward to it immensely; we shall
come out with it in about a week, and that is
also one of the things which makes my head in
a whirl just now, for these rehearsals, with all
the amateurs, ladies and gentlemen, singing and
screaming away all at once, and never keeping
quiet, are no easy matter. You are better off
at the Cæcilia Society, where they. have been
well drilled into obedience,—but then they
criticise among themselves, and that isn't nice

---

* Fink was the Editor of the *Allgemeine Musikalische Zeitung*, the
principal musical paper of the day. Schumann's was the *Neue Zeitschrift für Musik.—Ed.*

either. In fact—and so on ! I wish I were
at the Fahrthor — and also at the Pfarreisen,
you may believe me or not. Stamaty is staying
here, and I have got to teach him counterpoint—
I declare I really don't know much about it
myself. He says, however, that that is only
my modesty. And the carriage ! How am I
ever to thank you enough for it ? . .

Are you a Freemason ? People declare that
there are some four-part songs for men's voices
in the lodge here, which no one but a Freemason
could have composed. Do you still mean to
keep to your Italian journey in the spring ?
Pray, dear Ferdinand, write soon and long, and
forgive my silence, and don't punish me for
my small paper with a small sheet of your
own.

My best remembrances to your mother, and
write soon and keep well and happy.

Your Felix M. B.

A few weeks later I had this one :—

Leipsic, 26th November, 1836.

Dear Ferdinand,—Here is your Overture
(if you object to my having kept the autograph
I will bring it you at Christmas and exchange)

and the copies of your songs which you wanted, and which I went and got from Hofmeister. Many thanks for your delightful long letter, but now that I hope, please God, to be in Frankfort this day three weeks, I hardly feel in the mood to answer it properly. It is so much nicer and pleasanter to do it oneself in person. I should have sent you the Overture long ago, if the copyist had not kept me waiting such a shameful time ; the one in E will have to be repeated at one of the next concerts, and now I am curious to see what they will say to the D minor. As to the carriage, I may perhaps bring it back myself at Christmas. I am having it repaired a little, and the smith declares it will then be perfect. Many thanks to your mother for having lent it me. Stamaty will be at Frankfort in a few days, on his way back to Paris—I maintain that he has got *de l'Allemagne* and *du contrepoint double par dessus les oreilles* —and in three weeks, please God, I myself come to Frankfort. O that I were at the Pfarreisen! I should first come and say good evening to you, and then turn to the right. To-day I can only say, *auf Wiedersehen!* Remember me to your mother.

Your Felix M. B.

I have very little to tell about the short visit which he paid his *fiancée* at Christmas, excepting that I saw him oftener than might have been expected under the circumstances. He interested himself much in our work at the Cæcilia Society, where they had begun studying "St. Paul" under my direction. Our performance of it was the first after that at Leipsic, which Mendelssohn himself had conducted, though in reality the third, counting that at the Düsseldorf Festival, while the work was still in manuscript.

Shortly after his return to Leipsic I received the following letters :—

LEIPSIC, 10*th January*, 1837.

DEAR FERDINAND (OLD DRAMA),—First let me thank you for the *nervos rerum* which you lent me, and which I now return ; they were of the greatest service, for I had very little left when I got here. Still I don't think that that was the chief reason why I felt so dreadfully low when I came into my room again on the evening of my return—so low, that even you with your flinty heart would have pitied me ; I sat quite quiet for full two hours, doing nothing but curse the Subscription Concerts to myself. And with this

old strain I come back to Hafiz, and wish I were
at the Pfarreisen. I am always happy there.
Tell me yourself, what pleasure *can* I take in
the remaining nine concerts, in the Symphony
by H. and the Symphony by S. ? The day after
to-morrow we have Molique's Symphony, and
that is why I am writing to you, because we had
to put off your Overture till the next concert,
when we shall also have [Sterndale] Bennett's
pianoforte * concerto, the sacrifice scene from
" Idomeneo," and Beethoven's B flat symphony.
I meant not to write before next Friday, but
as that would put it off for a week, and I want
to save my reputation as a man of business, I
will write again then. So you had better look
out and answer me before that, or I shall abuse
your Overture, or rather, make it go badly, and
intrigue against it, *secundum ordinem Mel-
chisedek*, etc. . . . You once praised me for
making friends of all the German composers,
but this winter it's the very reverse—I shall be
in hot water with them all. I have got six
new symphonies lying here ; what they are like
God only knows, I would rather not ; not one
of them will please, and nobody has to bear
the blame but me, because I never let any com-

---

* Concerto No. 3, in C minor, played by the composer himself. —*Ed.*

posers but myself have a chance, especially in symphonies. Good heavens! Ought not the Capellmeisters to be ashamed of themselves, and smite their breasts? But they spoil everything with their cursed artistic consciousness and the wretched "divine spark" which they are always reading about.

When am I to have my pianoforte piece, "Drama"?

I have sent my six Preludes and * Fugues to the printer to-day; they will not be much played, I fear; still I should very much like you to look them through some time, and tell me if anything pleased you in them, and also anything to the contrary. The Organ † Fugues are to be printed next month; *me voilà perruque!* I wish to goodness that some rattling good pianoforte passage would come into my head, to do away with the bad impression. Oh dear! I only really care about one thing, and that is the calendar. Easter falls early—I wish it would fall at once. However, I have informed my Directors that I must leave directly after the last concert (17th of March), and cannot conduct any oratorio, either my own or the Angel Gabriel's, because of family affairs. They

---

* For Piano. Op. 35.
† Three Preludes and Fugues for the Organ. Op. 37.—*Ed.*

understand this, and think it quite fair. If only I had not to wait so long. How many times must it thaw, and freeze, and rain, and must I be shaved, and drink my coffee in the morning, and conduct symphonies, and take walks, before March comes. Schumann, David, and Schleinitz (though he does not know you) wish to be remembered to you. I must leave off and go to dinner; in the afternoon we rehearse Molique, in the evening there is a fête for the newly-married couple (the Davids); his wife is really here, and is a Russian, and he is married to her, and is a brother-in-law of Prince Lieven, and our "Concertmeister." It is needless to say more. Many remembrances and good wishes to your dear mother, and many compliments de Mdlle. J. And so farewell, and do not forget your

Felix M. B.

Leipsic, *24th January,* 1837.

My dear Ferdinand,—I have to give you my report of the performance of your D minor Overture,* which took place last Thursday evening. It went very well; we had rehearsed it

---

* Afterwards published by Breitkopf and Härtel, with many alterations, under the title of "First Concert Overture in D minor, Op. 32."

very carefully several times, and many parts of it greatly surpassed my expectations; the most beautiful of all is the A minor *piano* passage in the wind, and the melody that follows it—it sounds capital; then also, at the beginning of the so-called working-out, the *forte* in G minor, with the *piano* after it (your own favourite passage), and then the drums and wind instruments *piano* in D major right at the end. The winding-up sounds far better in the orchestra than I had expected. But I must tell you that after the first rehearsal, relying on the good understanding between us, I could not resist changing the basses to the melody in A—and also where it comes back in F and in D—from *staccato* to sustained notes; you can't think what' a restless effect it had before, so I hope you won't be annoyed at my taking such a liberty; I am convinced you would have done the same, for it did not sound at all as you wanted it to.

But now, there is still something on my mind which I want to say. The Overture, even at the performance, did not take hold of the musicians as I had wished, but left us all a little cold. This would not have mattered, but it was remarkable that all the musicians whom I spoke to, said the same—they had all been extremely

pleased with the first subject and the whole of
the opening, and the melodies in A minor and
major, and so far had felt quite worked up by
it, but from that point their liking began to
decrease, till by the end, the good and striking
impression of the subject was forgotten, and they
felt no more interest in the music. This seems
to me important, for it touches again upon a
matter about which we have had such endless
discussions, and the want of interest with which
it is possible for you at any time to regard your
art, must at last be felt by others also. I
would not like to say this to you if I were not
so perfectly convinced that the point is just
one at which every man is left to *himself*, and
where neither nature, nor talent, not even the
very greatest, can help him, but only his own
will. I dislike nothing more than finding fault
with a man's nature or talent; it only depresses
and worries and does no good; one cannot add
a cubit to one's stature, all striving and
struggling are useless there, so one has to be
silent about it, and let the responsibility rest
with God. But in a case like the present with
your work, where all the themes, everything
which is talent or inspiration (call it what you
will) is good and beautiful and impressive, and
the development alone not good, then I think

it may not be passed over; there, I think that blame can never be misplaced,—that is the point where one can improve oneself and one's work; and as I believe that a man with splendid capacities is under an obligation to become something great, and that it may justly be called his own fault if he does not develop himself exactly in proportion to the means given him, I also believe it ought to be the same with a piece of music. Don't tell me, it is so, and therefore it must be so; I know perfectly well that no musician can make his thoughts or his talents different to what Heaven has made them; but I also know that if Heaven has given him good ones, he must also be able to develop them properly. And don't go and tell me that we are all mistaken, and that your treatment is always as good as your invention; I don't think it is. I do think that as far as talent goes you are equal to *any* musician of the day, but I know hardly any piece of yours which is satisfactorily worked out. The two Overtures are certainly your best things, but the more clearly you express yourself, the more one feels what is wanting, and what in my opinion you ought to remedy.

Don't ask me, how; for you know that best yourself; after all it is only the affair of a walk, or a moment—in short, of a thought. If you laugh at me for all this long story, you will perhaps be doing very right; but certainly not, if you are angry, or bear me a grudge for it,—it is foolish of me even to think of such a thing; but how many musicians are there who would put up with it from another? And as you must see from every word how I love and admire your talent, I may also say that you are not perfect—and that again would offend most musicians. But not you, for you know I take the matter to heart.

As for that passage in Bach, I don't happen to have the score, and I should not be able to find it here at once, but I never considered it a misprint, though the edition generally swarms with them. Your version seems to me therefore incorrect. I should have thought the A flat quite necessary at "Thou smotest them"—and peculiarly Bach-ish.

Kindest regards. Your F. M.

This letter, in which Mendelssohn lectures me so affectionately, appears in the second volume of his published letters, but I felt that I could not omit it here; and I must add a few words, with regard to the matter about which

we had had "such endless discussions," as Felix
says,—a matter in which to this day I believe
myself to be right, though I do not therefore
by any means wish to set myself up against his
criticism on that occasion.

That a composer must be *born*—that unless
there is a natural power working in him with
all the force of instinct, he will produce nothing
of paramount greatness—there can be as little
doubt as that he must learn and study all that
is to be learned, quite as much and more than
he would do for mere technical purposes. But
the question now arises, where does the inborn
power end, and the power of workmanship begin?
According to Mendelssohn's opinion, as expressed
above, all that comes within the range of invention of melody belongs to the first power, and
the development to the second, in which the
strong will, coupled with the presupposed amount
of ability and dexterity, deals like a master with
the material in hand. This view of his, no doubt
shared by many, had a twofold source, in his
harmonious nature and his perfectly matured
artistic education. The greater spontaneity of
melodious thought cannot be denied ; and though
with the acceptance or rejection of the *first
inspiration* criticism already comes into play, the
choice in that case is not so *indefinite* as it

becomes in the *working out* of the leading ideas—
and choice is always distracting. But in spite of
this, it seems to me a mistake to consider the
after development as less dependent on original
genius than the first discovery; for if this development rests only on what has been learned and
studied, if the qualities of poetical creation do
not come into play in the same degree in both
cases, if it is not fresh, living, and original, it
cannot make any impression ; the cleverness and
learning of the musician will always meet with
due recognition, but can never make him pass
for an inspired composer. One might even assert,
that in the union of musical thought and specu-
lation with the vivid power of the imagination,
a still higher degree of productive genius is
called out than in the formation of the simple
melodious idea ; if indeed this latter, as soon as
it passes beyond the most elementary forms, does
not at once need the strongest chisel and the
finest file. I find the proofs of this opinion in
the masterpieces which adorn our art. In the best
works of the five great masters, Bach, Handel,
Haydn, Mozart, and Beethoven, it is impossible
to point out any separation between invention
and treatment; as soon as such a separation is
discernible, the music is no longer so great. In
fact, there are not a few cases where just the

whole force of genius shows itself in works
which have developed from comparatively unim-
portant germs; as, on the other hand, with
inferior composers, the working out and the
invention are much on the same level of poverty
and weakness. If there are some ingenious
composers, in whose works the "form" (a
word often used and generally mis-used) is not
on the same level as the subject-matter with
which they have been inspired, this is a want
which certainly lies more in their natural gifts
than in their education. For assuredly we are
attributing far too much to artistic education
and development if we can see nothing in natural
gifts, when they are in any way remarkable,
beyond the mere power of inventing melodies.
Amongst the countless gifts with which Nature
must endow the man whom she designs for a
great composer, one of the most essential is
a firm will to develop and deepen his own
ideas. It may sound hopeless to say that in
art this also is inborn; it is still more hopeless
to see many possessing it without the material
on which they might worthily employ it.

Mendelssohn, who was endowed with *all*
these gifts, only in less measure than the *very*
greatest of his predecessors, possessed also in a
preeminent degree that indefatigableness which

made him devote the minutest care, as well as the greatest energy, to attaining his ideal. He could not conceive that anything else was possible. And yet after all, towards the close of the letter just quoted, he himself admits, that the best must always be the half-unconscious; for what else—to use his own words—can be said to be " the matter of a walk, or a moment —in short, of a thought " ?

I need hardly add, that I have no wish to deny the necessity of the most uninterrupted, strenuous, and painstaking labour.

CHAPTER V.

MENDELSSOHN was married on the 28th of
March, the ceremony taking place in the French
Reformed Church, to which his bride belonged.
It seemed strange to hear anyone so thoroughly
German harangued in French on this solemn
occasion; but the simplicity of the service, and the
extraordinary fascination of the young couple,
touched and impressed everyone. I had composed
a marriage song for the reception of the newly-
married pair at the grandparents' house, and for
its performance had engaged the services of the
ladies belonging to a small choral society which
I had conducted every week during the winter
at the E.'s house. In spite of all the admiration
and idolatry of these young ladies for Mendelssohn, and though they knew we had leave,
and that it was very pretty and laudable to show
such an attention to so great an artist, it was
not without some embarrassment that the graceful

band entered the strange house under my direction, and took up their position in battle array
before the eyes of the astonished servants, to
await the expected arrival. But Mendelssohn and
his charming bride were so touched and pleased,
and the numerous members of the family, as
might have been expected, so extremely amiable,
that the fair singers soon completely forgot their
doubtful situation, and thoroughly enjoyed being
in the thick of the merry throng.

The young couple went first to spend some
time at the charming town of Freiburg-im-
Breisgau. A place more congenial to their poetic
and artistic tastes could hardly have been found.
It is a smiling little city, with clear streams
running through the streets, glorious hills looking
down on it all around, lovely environs with
views over mountain and valley, river and plain;
and besides all this, the homely, simple, South-
German dialect and manners—in short a perfect
place for a honeymoon. It will be remembered
that Cécile had great skill in painting. She
and Felix kept a journal,* unique of its kind,
which I was allowed to see on their return, and
which contains written matter and drawings by
each in turn, landscapes, houses, little scenes in

* Now in the possession of Mendelssohn's youngest daughter,
Madame Wach, at Bonn.

which they took part—in fact, hundreds of things done on the spur of the moment. During their absence I constantly heard news of their doings from the lively and communicative Madame Jeanrenaud. In the middle of May the happy pair returned to Frankfort. Felix writes in a letter to Devrient :—"I can only tell you that I am perfectly happy and in good spirits, and though I never should have thought it, not the least over-excited, but just as calm and settled as if it were all quite natural." In this tranquil happy state I found him on his return. But when he showed me the 42nd Psalm,* the musical result of his wedding tour, I was astonished—though only so long as I had seen nothing but the title. For the tender and longing pathos which pervades some parts of it is based on a foundation of perfect trust in God, and the subdued sentiment which for the most part characterizes the work, may well harmonize with the blissful feelings of deep happiness which penetrated him at the time. The final chorus, the words of which do not belong to the Psalm, and which he composed afterwards at Leipsic, seems to me not entirely in keeping with the other movements.

---

* (Op. 42.) "As the hart pants."

However, I must at once protest against the possible misunderstanding of my being supposed to hold artistic creation in general to be the produce of the state of mind at the moment. Even in the most ordinary life the mood of the mind changes so continually, that if one were to follow it, no artistic work of any unity would ever come into being; these matters are ruled by other and higher laws. But anything which was the result of such a wedding tour naturally leads one to make observations and draw comparisons, though I should hardly have expressed them if they had not forced themselves upon me at the time.

In the midst of the engagements and excitements which now engrossed the young pair, Felix composed his beautiful E minor quartet,* the progress of which I watched with the keenest interest. I must not forget one of the last occasions on which I conducted the Cæcilia Society. The performance was in honour of the young couple, and consisted chiefly of selections from "St. Paul," with pianoforte accompaniment only; and I remember how delighted Mendelssohn was with the fine rendering of some of the

---

* Op. 44, No. 2. The Autograph is dated "18th June, 1837, Frankfurt."—*Ed.*

chorales, which I had made the chorus sing *a capella*.

It was now almost time for me to set out on my Italian journey. Mendelssohn, meanwhile, travelled on down the Rhine, and we hoped to see him again in a few days. Our hopes were, however, disappointed, and my next letter from him was dated from Bingen :—

BINGEN, 13*th July*, 1837.

DEAR FERDINAND,—When you got into the carriage the other day at Homburg, and drove off with your ladies, I must have had a presentiment that we should not meet again for some time ; I felt almost sure we should not. It is strange enough that it has really turned out so ; I shall not return to Frankfort before my English journey, but in a week or ten days I go from here to Coblenz, and so on, slowly down the Rhine ; and in September, when I get to Frankfort for half a day, you will already be far away in the mountains, perhaps across the Alps. Who knows where and when we may meet again ? In any case, I hope, unchanged ; how much we should have had to talk about before the long separation : but the chief thing is that we must have a happy meeting some time or other.

I could not manage it differently, the journey here was rather a sudden affair, and I was quite prepared to find the inn as uncomfortable as the one in Homburg, and no lodgings to be had; in that case we should very soon have come back to Frankfort, and I should have betaken myself to the Hôtel de Russie. Contrary to our expectation we found the inn quite bearable, the view beautiful, and the neighbourhood and environs so splendid and varied, that after a few days I put off thinking about returning to Frankfort, and have now quite given it up, for I hope that my people will go on a little further with me. You really cannot think how this beautiful spot on the Rhine grows upon me every day, and how I love it; I have often seen it before, but only in a superficial way. In five minutes, with a boat, I am at the "Mäusethurm," my favourite point, and then over at Rüdesheim; and the Rhine is so beautiful in the changeable weather, and even after the late storms.

Thank God, my dear Cécile is well and cheerful; if I tell you that I love her more every day, you won't believe me, but it's literally true. I have not worked much here, I mean not written much, but I have a new violin quartet, all but finished, in my head, and I think I shall finish my pianoforte Concerto next week. I have

mostly followed your advice in the alterations
in the E minor violin quartet, and they improve
it very much ; I played it over to myself the
other day, on an abominable piano, and quite
enjoyed it, much more than I should have
imagined. And so one day passes like another,
but all are happy.

This letter is to remind you of our agreement that you should always write on the
15th of the month and I on the 1st. Do
let us keep to this, dear Ferdinand, even if
the letters contain only a few lines or words,
the regular correspondence is so precious. Please,
leave your E minor Symphony at the Souchays'
for me when it comes from Paris, so that I may
take it to Leipsic in September, I shall immensely
enjoy having a good look at it and hearing it
again properly. The Cæcilia Society wanted to
have another musical evening in your especial
honour, and I had promised to conduct ; but I
had to give that up too. Did anything come
of it after all ? And do all the musical heads
in Frankfort still show their teeth at one another?
And does —— show you his stumps ? This stupid
behaviour of the German musicians annoyed me
more even than I said at the time. But it is
God's will, so let the devil take them. Even
their daily life is a mere hell upon earth. And

H

so farewell; I have got back into the angry
style again after all.

My address till the 1st of August is here,
poste restante; from then till the 10th, Coblenz,
poste restante; from then till the 20th, Düsseldorf, ditto; from then till the 20th of September,
London, care of C. Klingemann, Hobart Place,
Eaton Square, Pimlico; and from the end of
September again in Leipsic. Is not that very
precise? And my pianoforte piece? Am I
ever to get it? Do tell me, for I should so
like something new and good to play, and can
hardly count on my concerto for that.

And now farewell, dear friend. Write to me
soon. Many many remembrances to your mother,
and thank her for the love and kindness which
she has so often shown me; think of me sometimes, and let us look forward to a happy
meeting soon.

Your Felix M. B.

I too at last set out on my journey, beginning
by wandering through the Black Forest on foot,
and spending some delightful days in Baden
with my friend Ferdinand David, also just
married, and his lively, refined, and interesting
wife. Thence I went to the Tyrol, and late in
the autumn to Italy, where I spent the winter,

and where my mother, who could not bear to be separated from me, joined me as soon as the weather began to get pleasant. Mendelssohn's letters to me during that time, some of which follow here, give a far better picture of the highly gifted man and true friend, than my pen can possibly do.

LONDON, 1*st September*, 1837.

DEAR FERDINAND,—Here I sit—in the fog—very cross—without my wife—writing to you, because your letter of the day before yesterday requires it; otherwise I should hardly do so, for I am much too cross and melancholy to-day. It's nine days since I parted from Cécile at Düsseldorf; the few first were quite bearable, though very wearisome; but now I have got into the whirl of London—great distances—too many people—my head crammed with business and accounts and money matters and arrangements—and it is becoming unbearable, and I wish I were sitting with Cécile, and had let Birmingham be Birmingham, and could enjoy my life more than I do to-day. D—n it! you know what that means, don't you? and I have three more weeks of it before me, and have got to play the organ at B. on the 22nd and be in Leipsic again on the 30th

—in a word, I wish I were rid of the whole business. I must be a little fond of my wife, because I find that England and the fog and beef and porter have such a horribly bitter taste this time—and I used to like them so much. You seem to be having a splendid journey, and this letter will see finer country than I do, as it has to go to Innspruck. Do inquire at Innspruck if anybody knows anything about a Herr Christanell of Schwatz, who has written to me twice, and calls himself a great amateur of music, and about whom I should like to know more. And so you are seriously thinking about your Jeremiah, and all the while striding off to Italy to compose operas there for the season? You really are a mad " old Drama."

It is pretty quiet here. Most people are away in the country or elsewhere. The Moscheles' have been at Hamburg for some weeks, and I shall not see them ; Thalberg is giving concerts at Manchester and other places ; he has made an extraordinary sensation and is very much liked everywhere, and I hope still to meet him ; Rosenhain is at Boulogne, and coming back soon ; Benedict at Putney, *à la campagne ;* Miss Clara Novello travelling from one Festival to another, and will probably not be in Italy until next spring ; till then she comes to Leipsic for our concerts (pray forgive me, I would willingly give her up to you, but—duty). I met Neukomm on the Rhine steamer, as polite and unapproachable as ever, and yet showing a friendly interest in me; he asked a great deal after you, &c., &c. Simrock promised to write directly, and put himself into communication with you about the manuscripts; I told him I did not know whether you had anything for him just at present, that it was more for the future. Has he written?

I have heard nothing from my people in Berlin for so long (more than five weeks) that I am beginning to be anxious—and that adds greatly to my unhappiness. I composed a great deal whilst we were on the Rhine, but I don't mean to do anything here but swear, and long for my Cécile. What's the good of all the double counterpoint in the world when she is not with me? I must leave off my complaints and my letter, or you will be laughing at me at Innspruck in the sunshine. Address to Leipsic again,—I wish I were there. It seems that Chopin came over here quite suddenly a fortnight ago, paid no visits and saw nobody, played very beautifully at Broadwood's one evening, and then took himself off again. They say he is still very ill and miserable. Cécile will

have given my remembrances to your people
herself. So farewell, dear "Drama," and forgive
this horridly stupid letter, it is exactly what I
am myself.

Your FELIX M. B.

The chief thing I leave for the P.S., just
as all girls do. Am I ever to get your E minor
Symphony? Do send it to me! You have
cheated me out of my concert piece. Get me
the E minor Symphony, the Leipzigers must
hear it—and like it.

LEIPSIC, 10th December, 1837.

MY DEAR FERDINAND,—I thank you with all
my heart for having written in November,
in spite of my last month's irregularity; I
really could hardly have believed it. The
arranging of my new house, moving into it,
with many concerts and a deal of business—in
short, all the impediments, whatever they may
be, which a regular Philistine, like I, can only
enumerate to a smart and lively Italian like you
—my installation as master of the house, tenant,
musical director of the Subscription concerts—all
this prevented me from doing my regular correspondence last month. But just because of that

I wanted to beg you, and I do beg you
to-day, most earnestly, that in spite of all the
inconceivable difference of our positions and surroundings, we should stick fast to our promise
of monthly letters ; I feel that it might be
doubly interesting and good for us both to hear
about each other, now that we must seem so
dreadfully strange to one another, and yet just
for that reason all the closer friends. At least
I find that whenever I think of Milan and Liszt
and Rossini, it gives me a curious feeling to
remember that you are in the midst of it all ;
and with you in the plains of Lombardy it is
perhaps the same when you think of me and
Leipsic. But next time you must write me a
long detailed letter, full of particulars, you
can't imagine how they interest me ; you must
tell me where you live, what you are writing,
and everything that you can about Liszt
and Pixis and Rossini, about the white cathedral,
and the Corso—I do so love that enchanting country, and it's a double pleasure to
hear from you from there, so you really
mustn't use half-sheets. Above all, tell me if
you enjoy it and revel in it as thoroughly as
I did ? Mind you do, and mind you drink in
the air with as much ecstasy, and idle away
the days as systematically as I did—but why

should I say all this, you will do it anyhow?
Only please write me a great deal about it.

You want to know whether I am satisfied
here? Just tell me yourself if I oughtn't to
be satisfied, living with Cécile in a nice, new,
comfortable house, with an open view over the
gardens and the fields and the city towers, feeling
so serenely happy, so calmly joyful as I have
never felt since I left my parents' house, and
able to command good things and goodwill on
all sides! I am decidedly of opinion, either this
place or none at all. I felt this very strongly
after the reports about ——'s place at ——;
no ten horses and no ten thousand thalers could
take me there, to a little court, which from its
very smallness is more pretentious than the great
ones, with the utter isolation of its petty musical
doings, and the obligation to be there the whole
year managing the theatre and the opera, instead
of having my six months free. However there
are also many days when I think *no* post would
be the best of all. Two months of such constant conducting takes more out of me than two
years of composing all day long; in the winter
I hardly get to it at all. At the end of the
greatest turmoil if I ask myself what I have
actually been doing, after all it is hardly worth
speaking of, at least it does not interest me

particularly whether or not all the recognized
good things are given one time more or better.
I only feel interested in the new things,
and of these there are few enough. I often
think I should like to retire completely, never
conduct any more, and only write; but then
again there is a certain charm in an organized
musical system, and in having the direction
of it. But what will you care about this in
Milan? Still I must tell you, if you ask
me how I like being here. I felt the same
thing at Birmingham; I have never before
made such a decided *effect* with my music
as there, and have never seen the public so
entirely taken up with me alone, and yet there
was something about it, what shall I call it?
something flighty and evanescent, which rather
saddens and depresses than encourages me. It
so happened that there was an antidote to all
these eulogies, on the spot, in the shape of
Neukomm; this time they ran him down wholesale, received him in the coldest way, and completely set him aside in all the arrangements,
whereas three years ago they exalted him to the
skies, put him above all other composers, and
applauded him at every step. You will say that
his music is not worth anything, and in that no
doubt we agree; but still, those who were enrap-

tured then, and now affect such superiority, do
not know that. I am indignant about the whole
affair, and Neukomm's quiet, equable behaviour
appeared to me doubly praiseworthy and dignified when compared to theirs. This resolute
demeanour of his has made me like him much
better. Just fancy also that I had to go straight
from the organ loft into the mail coach, and
drive for six days and five nights on end till I
got to Frankfort, then on again from there the
next day, arriving here only four hours before
the beginning of the first concert. Well then,
since that we have given eight concerts, such
as you know, and the " Messiah " in the church.
Our star this winter is Clara Novello, who has
come over for six concerts, and has really delighted the whole public. When I listen to that
healthy little person, with her pure clear voice,
and her animated singing, I often think of how
I have actually stolen her away from you in
Italy, for she was going straight there, whereas
now she will not go till the spring. But by
persuading her to come here I was able to do
our cause the greatest service, for this time it
is she alone who puts life and spirit into it, and
as I said before, the public are wild about her.
The air from " Titus " with *corno di bassetto*, the
Polacca from Bellini's " Puritani," and an English

Air * of Handel's, have driven the public quite frantic, and they swear that without Clara Novello there is no salvation. She has her whole family with her, and very pleasant people they are. You are often and much thought of.

The finest of the new things was Beethoven's "Glorreicher Augenblick," a long Cantata (three-quarters of an hour, with choruses, solos, etc.) in honour of the three monarchs who met at the Vienna Congress ; there are splendid things in it, amongst others a Cavatina,—a prayer, quite in Beethoven's grand style, but with wretchedly stupid words, where "heller Glanz" is made to rhyme with "Kaiser Franz," followed by a great flourish of trumpets ; and now Haslinger has actually put other words to it, and calls it "The Praise of Music," and these are even more wretched, for "poesy" is made to rhyme with "noble harmony," and the flourish of trumpets comes in still more stupidly. And so we spend our days in Germany.

David played my E minor quartet in public the other day, and is to repeat it to-day "by special desire ;" I am curious to know how I shall like it ; I thought it much prettier last time than I did at first, but still I do not care much about it. I have begun a new one which

---

* "From mighty kings."—Judas Maccabæus.—*Ed.*

is almost finished, and which is better. I have also done a few new songs, some of which would probably please you, but my pianoforte Concerto I think you would challenge. It's your own fault, why haven't you sent me your promised piece? You perhaps don't know that Ricordi, the music-seller, often sends parcels here to Wilhelm Härtel. So you might put it in some day. There's a delicate reminder! I have had to get the score of your E minor * Symphony written out from the parts; the score that came with it (in your own hand) had an almost totally different first movement, the *Andante Allegretto* was in B flat instead of C, and the two last movements quite different,—in short I did not know what to do, and only yesterday had the pleasure of receiving the old well-known score from the copyist and playing it through at once. I have put it down for one of the January concerts, and it will form the second part by itself. The two middle movements are quite superb. Now I must stop. Give Liszt many remembrances from me, and tell him how often and with what pleasure I think of him. Remember me to Rossini, if he likes being remembered by me. And above all, keep fond of me yourself.

Your FELIX.

---

* This Symphony has not been printed.

LEIPSIC, 20*th January,* 1838.

You Milanese "Drama," you begin your letter
so contemptuously, and look down so upon my
reminder about punctuality, that I had almost
resolved, first to be very punctual myself, and
secondly not to remind you any more.   But
as you may see from the date that I have not
kept the first resolution, I also cannot answer for
keeping the second or slipping a reminder into
this letter now and then—you may attend to
them or despise them, as you like; I am past
improvement you see (I mean, "incorrigible").
But joking apart, I should have written to you
at the New Year, and thanked you for your dear
good wishes, and given you mine, but I was
prevented in the most tiresome way by an indis-
position or illness, which attacked me in the last
week of the year and I am sorry to say has not
yet subsided.   This has put me into bad spirits,
and at times made me so desperate, that even
to-day I only write because I see that it is no
use waiting till I am better.   I am suffering, as
I did four years ago, from complete deafness of
one ear, with occasional pains in the head and
neck, &c. ; the weakness in the ear keeps on
without any interruption, and as I had to conduct and play in spite of it (I have been keeping

my room for a fortnight) you may imagine my agony, not being able properly to hear either the orchestra, or my own playing on the piano! Last time it went off after six weeks, and God grant that it may do the same this time; but though I summon up all my courage, I cannot quite help being anxious, as, till now, in spite of all remedies, there is no change, and often I do not even hear people speaking in the room.

Besides this there is another still greater anxiety, from which I hope every day to be released, and which does not leave me for a moment. My mother-in-law has been here for a fortnight, you know for what reason. When you see your whole happiness, your whole existence, depending upon one inevitable moment, it gives you quite a peculiar sensation. Perhaps I shall be better when the weather improves; I hardly remember such a winter; for a whole fortnight we have had from 14 to 22 degrees of cold, yesterday at last it was milder, but we had a snowstorm, which is still going on and has almost blocked up the streets. How is it with you in Milan?

A thousand thanks for the details in your last letter, they interest me more than you can imagine, living as you do in the very midst of so much that sounds quite fabulous here. You must tell me a great deal about it all whenever

you write; tell me about your Psalm, and how
they sang it, and whether you have already
begun the opera, and what *genre* you have
chosen, and about Pixis' *début*—in short, all
about what you are doing and what you like.
Here everything goes on in the usual quiet
musical way. We have one subscription concert
every week; and you pretty well know what we
do there. For the New Year, when the concert
always opens with sacred music, we performed
my Psalm "As pants the hart."   I have written
a new and very elaborate chorus as a *finale* to it,
and the whole Psalm pleased me a good deal,
because it is one of the few things of my own
which I am as fond of now as when I was
writing it.   A symphony by Täglichsbeck, which
was very much praised in Paris, and played at
the Conservatoire, made but little impression, and
seemed to me nothing particular.

Henselt the pianist was here shortly before
the New Year, and certainly plays exquisitely;
there is no question about his belonging to the
first rank, but it remains to be seen whether he
will be able sufficiently to master his German
anxiety and conscientiousness, that is to say, his
nervousness, so as to make himself generally
known, and play in London or Paris.   He
practises the whole day till he and his fingers

are so done up that in the evening when he
has to give a concert he is quite tired and
exhausted, and then, compared to other times,
plays mechanically and imperfectly. His great
specialty is playing wide-spread chords. He goes
on all day stretching his fingers, and amongst
other things does the following, *prestissimo* :—

His Studies are charming, and form a great
feature at his concerts. He is now off to
Russia.

We played your Overture in E at his concert;
it went well, and was greatly enjoyed. The Fernando Overture will come next; but your mother
did not send me the corrected score, only the
parts, which I did not want, because we have them
here. I got nothing but the score of the E
minor Symphony, which you said was to be
burned, but with your leave or without it I
shall do nothing of the sort. It is strange that
again I do not take to the last movement,
whilst the second and third please me even
more than before. It is fixed for one of the
February concerts. A symphony by Burgmüller
of Düsseldorf was very much liked the other

day. Yesterday Schleinitz brought me your
G minor song (in the "Europa"), sang it to
me, and made me guess whose it was; to my
great annoyance I couldn't, and was vexed with
myself afterwards, for I ought to have known
it by the beginning, and by the close in G
minor in the middle. In the way of new things
I have almost finished the violin Quartet,* and
also a Sonata for piano and cello,† and the day
before yesterday sent Breitkopf and Härtel six
four-part songs for mixed voices, small things
for singing in the open-air, or at parties.

The Novello, who has made *la pluie* and *le
beau temps* here, and at her farewell concert was
smothered with poems and flowers, and endlessly
applauded and shouted at, is gone to Berlin to
sing there; she passes through here again, and
will perhaps give us two more Arias, which
Leipsic has begged for on its knees—and is to
be in Italy by the spring, but in what part, I fancy
she knows at present as little as I do. She has
given the concerts a splendid impetus this winter,
and even if it is difficult to replace her, the
good effect will last for a time.

But what do you say to Ries's sudden‡ death?

---

* Quartet in E flat. Op. 44, No. 3.
† Sonata for piano and cello in B flat. Op. 45.
‡ Ferdinand Ries, Beethoven's pupil, died 13th January, 1838.—*Ed.*

It was a great blow to me, and gave me a strange feeling, just because his manner and way of going on had displeased me; but this news is such a contrast with all that, as to make one completely forget everything else for the moment. The Cæcilia Society certainly seems strangely fated. I have no idea who could or would undertake it now. Only a week ago Ries was slightly ill with gout and jaundice;—and in two days he is suddenly dead!

If you were in Germany now I should say you ought to go to Weimar in Hummel's* place; there must be much that is nice about it; perhaps it will remain vacant till you come back some day. You always liked Weimar very much. Above all, if you would only come back, there is no want of . places, I see that plainly now, it is only the men that are wanting—my old story over again. And you say that *you* are long past all that now. And I hope that *I* have not yet come to it.

Leipsic, 14th April, 1838.

Dear Ferdinand,—You will be angry with me for my long silence; again I can do nothing but beg pardon, and hope that your wrath will

---

* Hummel died 17th October, 1837.—*Ed.*

be changed into good-will when you see my
well-known fist. A great deal has happened
between this and the last letter, and much which
prevented me from writing. No doubt you have
heard through your mother that Cécile presented
me with a son on the 7th of February; but
perhaps you don't yet know that towards the
end of the month she suddenly became dreadfully
ill, and for four days and four nights had to
struggle with a terrible fever and all kinds of
other evils. Then she recovered, thank God,
quicker than could have been expected, though
still slowly enough, and it is only quite lately that
all traces of illness have disappeared, and that
she is again as cheerful and looks as well and
fresh as you recollect her. What I went through
at that time, I could not tell you in any letter,
nor indeed in words; but you will be able to
imagine it for yourself, dear Ferdinand. And
now that all the anxiety is over, and my wife
and child are well, I feel so happy, and yet not
a bit *philisterhaft*; you may laugh as much
as you like, I don't care, it is too lovely and
delightful to see a wee little fellow like that,
who has brought his mother's blue eyes and
snub nose into the world with him, and knows
her so well that he laughs to her whenever she
comes into the room; when he is lying at her

breast tugging away, and they both look so happy—
I don't know what to do with myself for joy. After
that I could decline *mensa*, or do finger exercises
with anybody for as long as ever they liked, and
allow you to laugh at me and welcome. In a
few days we go to Berlin, so that Cécile may
get to know my youngest sister and the whole
family; Paul and his wife were here last month,
and stood godfather and godmother to the little
one at his christening. The little man is called
Carl Wolfgang Paul. In Berlin I shall see how
my wife gets on at our house; if it's all right I
shall go by myself to the Cologne Festival in
four weeks, and come back directly afterwards to
Berlin, so as to spend the summer quietly there
or here and work. If not, Cécile will go with
me to Cologne ; but my mother and sisters
would not at all like that, so I think she will
probably stay with them, and perhaps go to the
Rhine with me next year.

These are my plans for the present. And
you ? If I were you I should certainly have
trudged off to Rome yesterday for Good Friday
and Palm Sunday, and I keep thinking that it
is still possible you may have done so. On
Palm Sunday I always think of the Pope's
chapel and the golden palm branches ; in the
way of ceremony and grandeur it is the most

solemn and splendid thing that I ever saw, and
I should like you to see it and think so too.
You do tell me capital things about Milan and
your life there ; how funny that you should find
your Paris circle there again — Liszt, Nourrit,
Pixis, &c. But it must all be intensely interesting, and I already look forward to the account
you are to give me at Leipsic some day of all
the " circumstances." You will have enough to
tell. And indeed you have hit off a horribly
truthful picture of the blissful happiness of a
Hofcapellmeister at ——, and the blissful patience
of the German public. I have had some
strange glimpses into that during the course of
this winter. For instance, in the case of the
post at ——, for which they wanted to get me
(probably because a couple of newspaper correspondents had said so), and where they have
again been using the most beautiful artifices to
make me *apply* for it, because they did not like
to speak straightforwardly and properly to a
musician ; however they were obliged to at last,
and in return I had the pleasure of most politely
refusing it, and so I see once more how right
you were with your dismal description. And
yet there is a certain something in this Germany
of ours—I hardly know what, but it has great
attractions for me, and I should like to con-

vince you. It is my old story over again,
which you have already heard two hundred
times, and have disputed four hundred times.
Certainly the theatre, as you describe it in
Italy, is better and has more life in it than
ours, but you should help us to bring about
an improvement. A. and his followers will
never do it, they only drive the cart deeper into
the mire, and will disappear without leaving a
trace.

But to turn to something better. Could you
and would you send me a copy of your Psalm?
and also any other new thing that you may
have, and give the whole parcel to Ricordi who
often sends things here to W. Härtel? That
would be splendid of you, and I beg you many
many times to do it. I too have been rather
busy this winter. David played a new violin
Quartet of mine, in E flat, in public the other
day at the last of his Soirées, and I think you
would find real progress in it; I have begun a
third; I have also finished a concert piece for
piano and orchestra (a sort of Serenade and
Rondo,* for of course I shall never get yours),
a new Psalm (the 95th),—I suppose I have
already written to you about my having added

* Serenade and Allegro giojoso for piano and orchestra (Op. 43).—*Ed.*

four numbers to the 42nd—and then there's a
set of four-part songs for open-air singing, and
various other little creatures that would so much
like you to clip and brush them a little if you
were here. *Apropos*, isn't this rich ? They have
been giving a first performance of my St.
Paul at Dresden, with all sorts of wonderful
preparations, and ten days before, R. writes me
a formal letter, saying that they wished to
shorten the first part a little, and he should
therefore cut out the chorus " Rise up, arise,"
with the chorale " Sleepers wake," as those
numbers did not appear to him to be necessary
for the action. I was stupid enough to be
frightfully put out for a whole day at this
piece of presumption, but you too will think it
rich.

Clara Novello will really soon be in Italy
now. I hear that she is at Munich, and will go
on from there direct. She went from us to
Berlin, where she had such incredible success,
that I am afraid it made her a little over-con-
fident, for at Dresden and Vienna, where she
went directly afterwards, she is said to have made
very little sensation. In Berlin, on the other
hand, she gave two concerts, sang twice for the
poor, four times at the theatre, twice at court,
and how can I tell where besides ? Mind you

pay her every possible attention, if she flutters
into your arms.

And now I must close, though I still have
quantities of things to say. More next time.
My wife sends you many best remembrances.
She is busy about the journey. Please write to
me to Berlin (Leipziger Strasse No. 3), then you
shall have Berlin news in exchange for Milan
news (by which I should lose a good many
yards). But good-bye, dear Ferdinand, be happy,
and always fond of your   F. M.

BERLIN, 15*th July*, 1838.

DEAR FERDINAND,—As all manner of creatures
were created by God, to wander about the earth,
bad correspondents among the number, don't be
too angry with me for having got this nature.
There are times when I cannot make the ink
flow, and if I could get answers (for instance
from you) without first writing myself, I really
should quite forget how to write. You may per-
ceive, first from my long silence and from my
present stiff writing, that this is one of those times.
But as I said before, it is for the sake of the
answer. I hope you will discover some quite new
way of abusing me for the beginning of your
letter, because then I am sure to get it soon.
And besides, you will have to answer as a man

of business, for I am writing on business, to ask
about the Overture which you promised us for
the concerts. What has become of it? I hope
we shall get it, and then we can at once put it
down for the beginning of the concerts (end of
September). Don't retort that I have not sent
you my things by Härtel's, as you wished; you
know that since then, I came here, and have been
leading rather a disturbed life, and besides, what
can you want with them now? I would rather
play them all to you *en gros* when you at last
come back to the Vaterland. But with you it is
different; because yours would be a help to me in
my performances, and would give us pleasure, and
you have promised it me, and I shall keep you
to your word. It is to be hoped the Overture
is finished, and it is also to be hoped that you
will send it. I feel more eager about it than I
have about any piece of music for a long time,
just as I do about your Italian life and doings
altogether. I fancy you now sitting by the lake
of Como with your mother; it must be a
delicious kind of life. And I suppose you also
go lounging about with Liszt, and paying court
to the Novello, who, I hear, is in Milan, taking
lessons; is she still your particular favourite?
What do you say to her singing, and to her
looks?

I have now been here in my old home since May. It gives me a peculiar sensation, so much in it is changed, so much in my own self is changed, and yet there is a sort of comfortable homelike feeling in it as if I had never left it. Then my family is so secluded and isolated here that one really knows very little of Berlin, and hardly comes into contact with anybody but the people in the house, which has its good side, as well as its disadvantages. Looking around me now as a stranger and free from prejudices, I certainly feel glad that I did not stay, however much I may regret it on account of my family; but the climate and the air here are unprofitable and good for nothing. For study and work and isolation Berlin is just the place, but hardly at all for enjoyment. Everything in my former life has now for the first time become quite clear to me, and I see plainly how all my old hostilities with the people and my bad position were brought about of necessity: and this has made these months especially interesting to me. We are quite pleased with each other now, and on the whole I like Berlin very much, because, having got rid of the wretched business altogether, I can enjoy what is good in the place without any bitter feelings.

The first evening after my arrival we went to

the theatre to hear Gluck's "Armida;" I have
hardly ever, if ever, enjoyed anything so much at
the opera. That great mass of thoroughly-trained
musicians and singers, ably conducted by Spontini,
the splendid house, full to suffocation, the good
mise-en-scène, and above all the wonderful music,
made such an impression on me that I was obliged
to say to myself that there was nothing to be
done with small towns and small means and small
circles, and that it was quite another thing here.
But how often since have I had to retract that.
The very day after, they gave a so-called Beethoven
Memorial Festival, and played his A major Symphony so atrociously, that I soon had to beg
many pardons of my small town and my small
means ; the coarseness and recklessness of the
playing were such as I never heard anywhere,
and can only explain to myself by the whole
nature of the Prussian official, which is about as
well suited for music as a strait-waistcoat is for a
man. And even then it is an unconscious strait-
waistcoat. Well, since then I have heard a good
deal in the way of quartets and symphonies, and
playing and singing in private circles, and have
altogether begged pardon of my little town. At
most places here music is carried on with the
same mediocrity and carelessness and assumption
as ever, which quite sufficiently explains my old

wrath, and the very imperfect methods I adopted to cure it. It all hangs together with the sand, the situation, and the official life, so that though one may enjoy a good thing here and there well enough, one cannot become really acquainted with anything. The Gluck operas may be reckoned amongst such good things. Is it not strange that they always draw a full house, and that the public applauds and is enchanted and calls the singers back? And that it is about the only place in the world where such a thing is possible? And that the next evening the "Postillon" draws just as full a house? And that in Bavaria it is forbidden to have any music in any church, either Catholic or Protestant, because it desecrates the church? And that *chorales* are becoming *obbligato* at the theatres? Confound it all.—— However the chief thing is to get as much novelty as possible, and that there should be plenty of good and beautiful things in the world; that is why I am so eager about your Overture and your Opera.

You will have heard that I was at Cologne for the festival. It all went well; the organ was splendidly effective in Handel and still more so in Bach—it was some newly-discovered music of his, which you don't yet know, with a grand double chorus. But even that, to my feeling at least, was wanting in the interest that one feels for something new and untried; I like so much when there is that kind of uncertainty which leaves room for me and the public to have an opinion; in Beethoven and Handel and Bach one knows beforehand what it will be, and must always be, and a great deal more besides. You are quite right in saying that it is better in Italy, where people have new music every year, and must also have a new opinion every year,—if only the music and the opinions were a little bit better. At this you snort and say : What *is* " better "? Well, if you want to know, something more to my taste. But really Germany seems to be possessed with the devil; Guhr has just been giving two tremendously brilliant performances of the " Creation "; all the newspapers are talking about the passage " Let there be light," where the bands of some Austrian and Prussian Regiments which Guhr had placed in the church, were made to blow their hardest. And the Cæcilia Society is conducted by V., who as far as I know is the best that they can get; and S. is making speeches in Mozart's honour, and all that is not to my taste. Perhaps after all my taste is perverted—the possibility of it occasionally dawns upon me—but I must make the best of it, though I certainly have about as much difficulty in swallowing most of these things, as the stork had with the porridge in the shallow dish. The stork reminds me of my boy, who is stout and fat and merry, and takes after his mother both in looks and disposition, which is an inexpressible delight to me, because it is the best thing he can do. Cécile is well and blooming and sends you many greetings.

But I have not told you anything about what I have been writing, I mean what music : two Rondos for Piano, one with and one without orchestra, two Sonatas, one with violin, the other with Cello, one Psalm, and just now I am at a third violin Quartet, and have a Symphony in my head, which will soon be launched. In B flat. And you ? Do you mean to send the Overture ? A thousand affectionate greetings to your mother. Enjoy your life in that heavenly country and think nicely of me.

Your F. M. B.

BERLIN, 17*th August,* 1838.

DEAR FERDINAND, — Your yesterday's letter delighted me so much, that I do not like to lose any time in telling you so. It is the nicest of all that I have ever had from you, and I

read it again and again, always with new delight
at the happy and tranquil mood which it
reflects, at each separate good and loving thing
in it, at the beginning and the middle and the
end. I am so glad that such happiness should
fall to your share, and I wish you joy of it with
all my heart, or rather I enjoy it with you, for
I see from your letter how well you know how
to enjoy it yourself. It must indeed be delightful there at Bellagio with your mother; and it
is because you seem so penetrated by this happy
feeling, that your letter gave me such pleasure,
for I confess I had hardly expected it. What
you tell me about the new Oratorio is also not
so bad, and I can see from all this that you are
just now living exactly the sort of life that I
always wished you to live, and about which I
was always holding forth to you—it's all the
same *where*—may Heaven keep it so for you
always, and may you always think of me
affectionately as you do in this letter.

The Babylonians certainly had valve trumpets
(in fact all Babylon was a kind of valve trumpet), such luxurious, arrogant Orientals would
hardly be satisfied with mere trumpets in C.
But please don't call them *trompettes à piston*
in your score, I have such a hatred for the word
piston—you see I am a regular doctor of phi-

losophy. Well, and when the Oratorio is finished,
are we to hear it in Germany ? Now, that will
really be a word in season. Only mind you do
it somewhere within my reach, so that I may
have some share in it, I mean in the first performance; you should do it in Leipsic, that would
be splendid, and all the singing and playing
faculties of the place should be at your command
and on their mettle for you. Do get it done
soon, and tell me a great deal about it, so that
I may at least have a foretaste of it in the
meanwhile.

I agree with every word you say about the
Novello, and also about Liszt. I am very sorry
that we are not to have the Overture, but of
course I can understand that you don't want
any of it to be played before the first performance. And will that be next winter ? And
is the whole Oratorio actually sketched out in
four parts ? That's really industrious, and by
this you at once set me an example, for the ten
operas and ten oratorios which you say I am to
write in the next twenty years. I assure you,
it gives me the greatest desire and stimulus to
follow your advice and example, if only there
were one true poet to be found in the world, and
he were my friend. It is too difficult to find so
much all at once. One would have to be driven

to it. Germany is wanting in such people, and that is a great misfortune. Meantime as long as I don't find any, I shift for myself, and I suppose one will turn up at last.

Your psalm with instrumental accompaniment and your wedding-chorus I received here, haven't I thanked you for them yet? It seems to me as if I had, and if I am mistaken I must tell you again how much pleasure you gave me with the latter, and what happy days are recalled by every note of the former. Your abridged Fernando Overture I received at Leipsic, and I think of giving it at the beginning of the Subscription Concerts; I shall write you all about it, and send it to you directly afterwards (at the beginning of November perhaps, if that is soon enough?) through Härtel and Ricordi. I shall add a couple of new things of my own; I wonder what sort of impression they will make upon you in Italy!

My time at Berlin is almost over now, and I think of going back to Leipsic in four days; they are going to do my St. Paul there in the church, and the rehearsals begin next week. Our family life here has been most pleasant; yesterday evening, when I went over to tea and found them all assembled, I read them a good deal out of your letter, which gave them

K

great pleasure, and they told me to give you many kind remembrances. We were together in that way every evening, talking politics, arguing, and making music, and it was so nice and pleasant. We only had three invitations the whole time, and of music in public I heard little more than I was obliged to; it is too bad, in spite of the best resources; I saw a performance of "Oberon" last week which was beyond all conception, I believe the thing never once went together all through; at the Sing-Akademie they sang me a piece of my own, in such a way that I should have got seriously angry, if Cécile had not sat by me and kept on saying: "Dear husband, do be calm." They also played me some quartets, and always bungled the very same passages that they had bungled ten years ago, and which had made me furious ten years ago—another proof of the immortality of the soul.

My third violin quartet, in D,* is finished; the first movement pleases me beyond measure, and I wish I could play it to you,—especially a *forte* passage at the end which you would be sure to like. I am also thinking of com-

---

* Op. 44, No. 1. The autograph, in possession of Sir W. Sterndale Bennett, is dated " Berlin, 24 July, 1838."—*Ed.*

posing an opera of Planché's next year; I have already got two acts of the libretto, and like them well enough to begin to set to work. The subject is taken from English history in the Middle Ages, rather serious, with a siege and a famine; I am eager the see the end of the libretto, which I expect next week. I also still hope to get words for an oratorio this year. You see, that I was already going to follow your advice of my own accord, but, as I said before, the aid and invention of the poet is wanting, and that is the chief thing. Pianoforte pieces are not exactly the things which I write with the greatest pleasure, or even with real success; but I sometimes want a new thing to play, and then if something exactly suitable for the piano happens to come into my head, even if there are no regular passages in it, why should I be afraid of writing it down? Then, a very important branch of pianoforte music which I am particularly fond of— trios, quartets and other things with accompaniment—is quite forgotten now, and I greatly feel the want of something new in that line. I should like to do a little towards this. It was with this idea that I lately wrote the Sonata*

---

* Sonata for piano and violin, in **F**—still in M S.

for violin, and the one for cello, and I am thinking next of writing a couple of trios. I have got a Symphony * in B flat in hand now, and mean to get it finished soon. I only hope that we shall not have too many foreign *virtuosi* at Leipsic this winter, and that I shall not have too many honours to enjoy—which means, concerts to conduct. So Herr F. has gone all the way to Milan. Brr, he is enough to spoil the warm climate. Yes, you see, I have to digest such creatures, and am in Leipsic, instead of at Cadenabbia, where I once was, opposite your present lodging. When I am writing to you at the lake of Como, I feel the greatest longing to see that paradise again, and who knows what I may do in the next year or two? But you will first have to have been here with your oratorio, which is best of all. Do you know that my sister Fanny will perhaps see you soon? She intends going to Italy with her husband and child and only returning next year.† When I know more definitely about her journey I will tell you, so that she may not miss you, as Franck did. Now good-bye, write to me soon

---

* Alas! this has never been published, nor is any MS. score, or any trace of it, beyond a few notes in memorandum books, known to exist.—*Ed.*

† See published letter to Fanny Hensel, of Sept. 14, 1839.

to Leipsic, just such another splendid letter.
Once more, thanks. Remember me to your
mother. Farewell, farewell.

Your Felix.

Leipsic, 15*th April,* 1839.

My dear good Friend,—I feel particularly
inclined to write to you to-day, and have a chat
with you; I was just thinking of how I used
to lie on your sofa and grumble and make you
play to me, because I was so much in love; and
then I thought, how nice it would be if we
could see one another again soon and really live
together, and then I thought what a long while
off that must be. But I have a lot of business
matters to write to you about to-day, and will
begin with them at once. First of all the oratorio.
What do you mean by talking about my "taking
responsibility upon myself" and the "risk of
looking through the score beforehand," &c.?
You insane fellow, as if I did not know all that
long before, and also how a work of yours which
you yourself take pleasure in and write with
real liking will turn out; and you know too
how I look forward to such a work, and that I
shall devote all the loving care that I can to
the performance of it, if you will entrust it to

me. Is it really necessary for me to tell you that first? However, that I might not follow my own opinion solely, or be alone in addressing you, I told the concert directors about the part of your letter referring to the oratorio (*cum grano salis*—that is to say, omitting your over-great modesty) and received the following answer from Stadtrath Porsche, the secretary to the concerts—at first I meant to send you the original letter, but I shall copy it instead, because the paper is so thick that the postage would be thick too :—

"Honoured Sir (notice the official style)—according to your obliging information that Herr Ferdinand Hiller is occupied at Milan in the composition of an oratorio, 'The Prophet Jeremiah,' from which great things may be expected as to merit and importance ; the concert directors have commissioned me to assure you that it would afford them much pleasure to see the work and hear it performed at one of the concerts during the coming winter of 1839-40, if Herr Hiller will have the kindness to forward the score to us. With the greatest esteem, etc., etc.,

"*Leipsic, March* 1839.　　　　PORSCHE."

It is to be hoped that you'll never think again about my having too much "responsibility."

And I hope that this insignificant opportunity
may give you zest and inclination for beginning a new work. In your next letter (addressed
to Düsseldorf till the middle of May, to Frankfort till the end of June) you must give me a
few words, in reply to this, which I may
communicate to the Directors; it pleases them
immensely when an artist like yourself takes
notice of them as the Committee of the Concerts,
and they were all much flattered by your
request. We could not well do it in the church,
because we shall have to let our church-concerts
rest for a year or two, before we can put them
on a proper footing again (it would take too
long to explain all the reasons), so it would be
in the concert-room, with a large chorus of
amateurs; therefore mind you give the chorus
plenty to do, and as I said before, answer as
soon as you can. There's a parcel going off to
you in a few days by Kistner; it has been in
his hands all ready packed for the last four
weeks, and at last he promises really to send it
off; it contains the score of my 42nd psalm,
"St. Paul," and a Cello sonata of mine lately
published (which I only send because of the
lovely cover, and by way of a novelty—otherwise there is not much in it). But if you are
not pleased with the psalm in its new dress with

the old lining, I shall shoot myself. The parcel
will be six weeks on the road, I hear, and will
be addressed to Giovanni Ricordi at Milan; so
you must inquire there when you have an
opportunity. Of course you understand that I mean
you to keep all the contents of the parcel.
I sent off your two overtures, with the metro-
nome marks, to the Philharmonic a fortnight ago,
after we had first given a good performance of
the one in D minor at the charity concert here,
and found your alterations very advantageous.
It gains very materially by them, and the flow
of it is not at all interrupted. And now, though
I am really ashamed to, I must tell you of an
article which I read about you in the newspaper
the other day, and which gave me a deal of
pleasure. One morning at rehearsal somebody
showed me a number of the new musical paper
(Schumann, the editor of it, was in Vienna all
the winter) in which there was something which
concerned me, and looking through the rest of
the paper, I found a leading article, continued
through two numbers, headed by your name. I
took it away with me to read, and a great deal
of it really gave me extraordinary pleasure; it
is evidently written by some one who is not personally acquainted with you in the very least
degree, but on the other hand knows every one

of your works most intimately, some one who was not even aware that you were no longer in Frankfort, and yet could picture you to himself quite well and distinctly from your compositions, and is evidently very favourably disposed towards you. I hear that it is said to have been written by a German in Warsaw. The real point of the thing is that he thinks that somehow or other you are out of humour, and have resolved not to publish or even compose anything more, and he implores you for Heaven's sake not to carry out this resolution, and not to believe that people do not watch you with sympathy and pleasure, as he does himself for example ; and the paper is headed with the motto : " How great the loss, when such heads make holiday." You see the writer knows nothing of you personally, but that was just why I enjoyed it, and I should have sent it to you if I had not almost sworn never to put newspaper extracts into my letters.

But this and a joke on the last page remind me of the too terrible and awful news of Nourrit's death. It is a long, long time since anything has grieved me so deeply and taken such strong hold of me as this. It made me think of the bright, happy time when I met him, of the genuine, free, artist-nature which he

seemed then to have, of the honour and glory
which he gained everywhere, of his wife and
children, and of the infinitely sad state of a
mind which knew no other remedy but one,
which wipes out the whole previous existence
with all its happiness as if it had never been.
How the news must have shocked you! It was
only in your last letter that you were speaking of
him; you had seen him so lately, and were so
fond of him—it is really dreadful. And who can
think of fame and celebrity and happiness, or wish
for them, when a man outwardly so happy and inwardly so gifted, could at the same time be
so boundlessly unhappy. To me, there is more in
it than in the profoundest sermon I ever heard,
and once I begin to think of it I cannot get over
it at all. Do tell me all you can about it; all
that you know of further particulars and details. I
have heard nothing but the details of the evening
before, and of his last moments. Tell me, if
you know anything about it, what could have
brought him to such terrible misery and to
such a resolve. If it were nothing more than
those few hissings and whistlings at the theatre,
as they say in the papers, nobody ought
ever to appear in public again after they
have once earned bread enough to keep them
from starving, or ought ever to choose a pro-

fession which would make them dependent on the public.

Now I must answer some of the questions in your letter. A number of different people conduct at the Philharmonic, Sir G. Smart, Moscheles, Potter, etc., so it is impossible to foretell into what sort of hands you might fall, clean or unclean. I am quite at sea again about my English opera; the poet won't alter it, and I won't compose unless he does—it's the old, old song of the drunken " Bohnenschmied." And I always have to begin it over again, because I know I am right. But woe betide you if you praise Mercadante's " Giuramento," for I have had the pianoforte arrangement in my room for ever so long, and have certainly given myself trouble enough with it, and yet I find it quite insufferable and vulgar, without a note in it which I care the least bit about. Don't be angry with me, I can't help it; it's curious that the surroundings and the air and the way it's done really do make an impression on everybody— but here in Leipsic the " Giuramento " cuts an awful figure—in my own house that is to say. You will never in all your life make music like that, it can't be; that is why I rejoice doubly for the numbers of your opera which you promise me and for which I am most eager.

In a week I go to the Festival at Düsseldorf, where the "Messiah" is to be given on the first day; on the second the "Eroica," the Beethoven C major Mass, an overture and my 42nd psalm; and on the third Gluck's "Alceste" in the theatre with costumes and all. There are to be singers from Berlin, and they will make the last (evidently the best) practicable. The festival is at Whitsuntide again. Afterwards we are to be at the wedding of my sister-in-law, Julie Jeanrenaud, who is going to marry a young Schunk from here; after that we stay on in Frankfort for a time, then spend a fortnight with my uncle on the Rhine—and my castles in the air go no further. Now this letter is really done; it's quite absurdly long; many many remembrances to your mother, and also to Mdlle. J., and write to me very soon, dear Ferdinand; your letters are such a pleasure to me.

Always your FELIX.

My wife and child are well and beg to be remembered to you.

FRANKFORT, 27*th June*, 1839.

MY DEAR FRIEND,—Your brother says I am to put in a word for you into his letter. Everything here, every day, every walk through the town and in the woods recalls you to me so strongly, that I ought long ago to have written you a proper letter of my own, and I mean to very shortly. I should like to write to you about all Frankfort, but that is just what keeps me from writing. So to-day I only send you and your dear mother my remembrances and best wishes. We are all well, and so is your brother and also your sister-in-law on the sofa in the next room. Your portrait over the sofa is like, after all, rather atrociously painted, but well conceived. Yes, if only you were here yourself. All your friends remember you most affectionately I can tell you, and all wish for you back again. It's to be hoped the oratorio will soon come now, and you with it, which will be far nicer than this letter paper and the 100 miles of separation.

Farewell for to-day, dear friend and musician; next time I shall write to you properly : forgive my haste and be a little fond of your FELIX.

FRANKFORT, 16*th* *August*, 1839.

MY DEAR FRIEND,—On returning here from Horchheim I find your letter from Basle, with the second part of the oratorio, and glancing

quickly over it in the bustle of travelling preparations, I am struck by so many and such
great beauties in it, that I can't help telling
you so to-day, though in few words, and thank-
ing you for the great pleasure and enjoyment
you have given me with it. This second part
seems to me far superior to the first in every
respect, and wherever I look I find splendid
touches, quite peculiar to you. What I like
best of all is the A major chorus with the
solo and the repeat—the *tempo*, and the
vigorous opening are new and capital; one
expects something quite different, and not nearly
so fine. And then the first chorus, and the war
march in C major, and the entrance of the
chorus in the recitative, and the one in F minor,
and in fact the whole thing. It seems to me
that the poet has again now and then missed
a point; but why should I begin criticising, when
there is so much to surprise and delight me
beyond my expectation? I promise you not to
open my mouth again, at least not till I get
your answer, which will be very soon I hope,
and till I know that you are not angry with me
for opening it so enormously wide already.
Write soon, dear Ferdinand, and thanks, thanks,
thanks for all this good and beautiful music.

Some letter of yours must have been lost. You

write that you may perhaps hear from me at
Bern, and I had no idea of your Swiss journey,
and was quite perplexed by your dating from
Basle. How shameful it is that we were so
near together, both on the Rhine, and now again
so far from one another! And yet it is quite
right that you should be in Italy again, and
that you should not let yourself be disturbed
in your wishes and doings. To-morrow I go
back to Leipsic, where I hope to hear from
you soon. My wife and child are well, and send
messages to you and your mother, and I do the
same with all my heart. Now I must be off.

I like your having put "Rigikulm, Midnight," at the end of the Oratorio; but the C
major is still better, and the A major opening
is the most beautiful of all, and so Ferdinand,
best thanks to you my dear friend.

Always your FELIX.

I had taken my dear mother and her companion to Basle, because the state of her health
made it necessary for her to take the baths at
Wiesbaden. Nevertheless, after a few weeks she
became so ill that I hastened home. I received
the following after I had written to Mendelssohn
from Frankfort about the anxieties which were
troubling me :

LEIPSIC, 19*th September,* 1839.

DEAR FERDINAND,—I need hardly tell you
how your yesterday's letter saddened me; you
know what heartfelt sympathy I feel in you
and your welfare. May God restore your dear
mother to complete health, and give comfort
and happiness to you all; I can well imagine
your anxiety and sadness at present; dear Ferdinand if only I were with you! Even though
I might not be able to help, I could perhaps
divert your thoughts a little; have I also not
felt from the bottom of my heart, how at such
moments all art and poetry and everything else
that is dear and precious to us, seem so empty
and comfortless, so hateful and paltry, and the
only thought that does one any good is: "Oh
that God would help." When you have a spare
moment, do write me a line to say how she
is; we should so much like to hear from you as
often as possible; write me a line at least every
week, I shall be so impatient for it.

I send off the first part of the oratorio by
to-day's post. I have not quite done with the
second, so I did not write to you in Italy about
it; I shall send it to-morrow or the day after,
and then write you properly and fully. Let us

hear from you again directly.   My wife sends best remembrances.

Your FELIX M. B.

My dear mother was not able to resist the illness which had attacked her, and died on the 22nd of September.

NOTE.

The subject of the Opera mentioned on page 131 was the Siege of Calais. For the correspondence between Mendelssohn and Mr. Planché, and the circumstances under which Mendelssohn at length decided to abandon it, see Mr. Planché's " Recollections and Reflections," Chap. XXI.

CHAPTER VI.

LEIPSIC, 29*th September*, 1839.

MY DEAR FRIEND,—No words are needed to tell you how deeply I grieve for you in this great sorrow; you know how I sympathize with you in everything that concerns you, whether it be good or bad, even in the merest trifles; how much more so then in the greatest loss which could befall you! Anyone who knew your dear mother in the very least, or had ever seen you together, must know what an irreparable blank is made in your life and heart by her death. But why say all this to you? I would so much rather be with you, so that we might have a quiet time together, and I might try and if possible help you to bear this bitter trial. Even that I cannot do; and besides, just at first, neither sympathy, nor words of comfort, nor even friends, can do one any good;

when they try their very best, they may
only do harm, and certainly cannot help or be
of any use; only God and one's sense of duty
can do that. But what I wanted to write to
you about was suggested to me by the last
words in your letter, where you say that you
must stay in Frankfort for the present on account
of business matters. When these are over,
couldn't you come to us for a little? Would
not the change of surroundings, the affectionate
and hearty welcome which you are sure of from
all the musicians here, the separation from a
place which though now doubly dear must also
be doubly sad, do you good, and if not cheer
you, at least distract your thoughts now and
then? I do not mean now directly, but I was
thinking of the end of next month, and November; my Vienna journey is as good as given up,
so I can offer you a nice, warm, pretty room,
which we would make as comfortable as possible
for you. Cécile joins with me in my request,
and we hope you will do what we ask.

I don't speak of how well we could talk
over the oratorio together, and all that we might
do towards arranging for the performance, or
of all the music that I should hope to make
you enjoy. To-day I only wish to impress upon
you how much I want you to spend the next

month in different surroundings, and with friends
who are as fond of you as we are.

How entirely our whole future rests always,
and every day, in God's hands ! My Cécile is
expecting her confinement in the next few weeks,
and if one is to speak of the cares of married
life, I as yet only know those which at such a
time engross me every hour and minute, and
leave me no peace for any other thought. Thank
Heaven, she is so well and strong, that I hope
God will continue to grant her health and happiness—and so with a sanguine heart I repeat
my request and our invitation to you. Farewell
for to-day, my dear, dear friend ; try to keep
up, and may Heaven give you courage and
strength !

　　　　　　　　　　Always your F. M.

In the course of a few weeks this affectionate
letter was followed by another similar to it, with
these words : " Your room is ready for you,
with a piano in it, and you shall be as undis-
turbed as you like ; and a good deal disturbed
too. My Cécile sends you her remembrances,
and joins most heartily in my request ; so do
come and try perfect rest and our quiet homely
life for a time, and let me hope to see you very
soon." It was impossible to resist such an invita-

tion, so I set off as soon as I could manage it.
I stopped at Weimar to pay a visit to the widow
of my revered master, Hummel, for she had
always been like a mother to me. There I
found the following lines from my thoughtful
friend :—

LEIPSIC, 3rd *December*, 1839.

DEAR FERDINAND,—As there was no time
after receiving your dear and welcome lines to
write to you at Frankfort, I send this to
Weimar, in the hope that you may get it immediately on arriving. I live in Lurgenstein's
garden, the first house on the left, on the
second floor. Let me know whether you travel
in your own carriage, or by post, so that, in
the first case, I may secure a place for your
carriage. Write me two lines from Weimar to
say when you are coming, and if possible tell
me the exact time of your arrival here, or
departure from there, then I can go and meet
you on the road. I need not tell you how
much my wife and I look forward to seeing you,
you dear friend. For the last three weeks all
our friends, and all the friends of music, have
kept on asking me, " When is Hiller coming ? "
and I have often had to tell them of your reso-

lution to keep quiet, so that they might not be too eager in their demands. Now good-bye till we meet!

Your Felix.

Mendelssohn and David met me at the place where the coach stopt and gave me the warmest of welcomes. In the course of the first few days. I was introduced to Mendelssohn's relations and friends, and soon felt as if I had belonged to that delightful circle for years. Mendelssohn's house was pleasantly situated, with a nice open look-out from the front upon the Leipsic boulevard, and the St. Thomas's school and church, once the sphere of the great Bach's labours. The arrangement of the rooms was as follows :— first, a sort of hall, with the dining-table and a few chairs : to the right of this a large sitting-room and some bed-rooms ; to the left my friend's study with his piano. Opening out of this was a fine large drawing-room, which however was robbed of some of its natural elegance by the bed which had been put there for me, though this was counteracted by a piano also put there for my use.

Our way of life was regular and simple. At about eight we breakfasted on coffee and bread and butter. Butter Felix never eat, but broke his bread into his coffee like any schoolboy, "as he had been accustomed to do." We dined at one, and though he despised butter he always liked a glass of good wine, and we often had to try some special sort, which he would produce with great delight, and swallow with immense satisfaction. We generally made quick work with our dinner, but in the evenings after supper we used often to sit round the table for hours chatting (not smoking), unless we moved to the pianino which had been presented to Madame Mendelssohn by the directors of the Gewandhaus.

The first few days were taken up with paying and receiving visits, and passed quickly enough. My next thought was to resume my work. I had a performance of my oratorio in prospect, and there was still a great deal to be done towards it. "We must sit and compose at the same table together," said Mendelssohn, one morning; "and let's begin at once to-day."

The following day was the Liedertafel, by which I must not be supposed to mean one of those huge societies formed in the last forty years to assist the love of the Vaterland and of "wine and woman." This one consisted of a dozen thorough musicians, some of them still representing the most zealous supporters of music in Leipsic, who used to meet from time to time, and did all honour to their title, for their *table* was no less excellent than their songs.* Mendelssohn thought it would be great fun if we set the same words to music, and let the singers guess which was which. No sooner said than done. We looked through several volumes of poetry, and soon agreed in the choice of a song of Eichendorf's. I can still see the two sitting opposite each other, dipping our pens into the same inkstand, the silence only broken at rare intervals by some joke or other, and the piano not once touched. In writing out the parts, each copied half of his own composition and half of the other's. The scores were not to appear, and above all the secret was on no account to be betrayed to the members of the Liedertafel.

The evening arrived, and the thing was a complete success. The songs were sung at sight in capital style, and only one of the singers, Dr. Schleinitz, one of the most accomplished of living amateurs, gave his opinion, with thorough conviction—and was right. None of the others could make up their minds. We laughed and— held our tongues.

Mendelssohn afterwards apologised to me—

---

* One of them, Dr. Petschke, has published some very pretty quartets for men's voices.

quite unnecessarily—for having let out the secret
by publishing his song.* I then published
mine in a Swiss collection, to which I had been
asked to contribute; I forget the title of it,
and where it appeared, but the origin of this
little piece was always a charming recollection
to me.

Though I had felt no difficulty in throwing
off a simple song in my friend's presence, it was
quite different with more serious work. It was
impossible to feel at ease at the piano, with
the consciousness that every idea had a listener,
and such a one! Besides, I afterwards discovered, by chance, that Mendelssohn equally
disliked his communings with his genius to be
overheard. How could it have been otherwise?
Still, I found it extremely difficult, in the midst
of much kindness and affection to come forward with the announcement, that, delightful as
was our way of life, it must come to a stop.
After many discussions, I at last got permission to look out for a lodging close by,
on the condition that I should only work and
sleep there; and to our general satisfaction we
found one within a few steps. They were the
same rooms in Reichel's garden which Mendels-

* "Love and Wine," Op. 50, No. 5.

sohn had inhabited in his bachelor days. So, after about a fortnight at my friend's house, I moved into my new quarters.

We had had a tolerable quantity of music, however, during this time. Mendelssohn had just finished his great D minor trio, and played it to me. I was tremendously impressed by the fire and spirit, the flow, and, in short, the masterly character of the whole thing. But I had one small misgiving. Certain pianoforte passages in it, constructed on broken chords, seemed to me— to speak candidly—somewhat old-fashioned. I had lived many years in Paris, seeing Liszt frequently, and Chopin every day, so that I was thoroughly accustomed to the richness of passages which marked the new pianoforte school. I made some observations to Mendelssohn on this point, suggesting certain alterations, but at first he would not listen to me. " Do you think that that would make the thing any better?" he said. " The piece would be the same, and so it may remain as it is." " But," I answered, " you have often told me, and proved to me by your actions, that the smallest touch of the brush, which might conduce to the perfection of the whole, must not be despised. An unusual form of arpeggio may not improve the harmony, but neither does it spoil it—and it becomes more interesting to

the player." We discussed it and tried it on the
piano over and over again, and I enjoyed the
small triumph of at last getting Mendelssohn
over to my view. With his usual conscientious
earnestness when once he had made up his
mind about a thing, he now undertook the
lengthy, not to say wearisome, task of rewriting
the whole pianoforte part. One day, when I
found him working at it, he played me a bit
which he had worked out *exactly* as I had suggested to him on the piano, and called out to
me, " That is to remain as a remembrance of
you." Afterwards, when he had been playing
it at a chamber concert with all his wonderful
fire, and had carried away the whole audience,
he said, " I really enjoy that piece ; it is honest
music after all, and the players will like it,
because they can show off with it." And so it
proved.

In the course of that winter I witnessed a
curious example of Mendelssohn's almost morbid
conscientiousness with regard to the possible perfection of his compositions. One evening I came
into his room, and found him looking so heated,
and in such a feverish state of excitement, that
I was frightened. " What's the matter with
you ? " I called out. " There I have been sitting
for the last four hours," he said, " trying to alter a

few bars in a song (it was a quartet for men's
voices) and can't do it."

He had made twenty different versions, the
greater number of which would have satisfied
most people. "What you could not do to-day
in four hours," said I, "you will be able to do
to-morrow in as many minutes. He calmed
down by degrees, and we fell into such earnest
conversation that I stayed with him till very
late. Next day I found him in unusually good
spirits, and he said to me, "Yesterday evening
when you were gone I was so excited that it
was no use thinking of sleep, so at last I composed a little hunting-song, which I must play
you at once." He sat down to the piano, and
I heard the song, which has since delighted
hundreds and thousands of people, namely Eichendorf's, "Sei gegrüsst du schöner Wald!" I
hailed it with joyful surprise.

Musical life in Leipsic, which has always
been extremely active, had certainly acquired an
extraordinary impetus through Mendelssohn's personal influence and energy. His eminent talent
as a conductor was especially favourable to the
performance of orchestral works. Vigorous leaders
had managed, before his time, by the help of
their fiddling, to put plenty of spirit and precision
into them, but no one had ever imagined so

deep a conception, or such artistic finish in
the performances of the great symphonies. It
was altogether a capital orchestra, though the
only example of extraordinary talent in it was
Ferdinand David, who followed the conductor with
his whole soul, and carried the whole of the
strings along with him. Having for many years
attended the (wrongly so-called*) Conservatoire
Concerts in Paris, I was naturally at first much
struck by the contrast, especially in the wind,
and the general tone and effect. At that
time the Leipsic Conservatorium was not yet
founded, and it was only afterwards that the
Gewendhaus Orchestra gained such material and
brilliant reinforcements from David's pupils. But
all the little imperfections in individual execution
were thrown into the background by the spirit
and life which Mendelssohn instilled into the
orchestra, his complete devotion to the cause,
and the delight which lit up his expressive features at every successful achievement, and acted
like electricity upon the public. When I speak
of his conducting thus influencing the audience,
it must not be supposed that he in any way
courted notice by his behaviour at the desk. His

---

* The name of the Institution is "Société des Concerts," and it
consists of the best musicians in Paris. The Conservatoire, as such, only
supplies the concert room, and the Sopranos and Altos for the chorus.

movements were short and decided, and generally
hardly visible, for he turned his right side to the
orchestra.   A mere glance at the first fiddle, a
slight look one way or the other, was sufficient.
It was the sympathy in the cause, which gathered
strength from the sympathy brought to bear on
it by so wonderful a man.

Symphonies and overtures were then, as now,
the prominent features in the Leipsic programmes.
It is well known what a ready welcome Mendelssohn had for any composers whose works in
any way deserved it.   Thus, in that winter, or
rather in the second half of it, many novelties
were produced.   Kalliwoda conducted one of his
symphonies (in B minor) which met with a very
favourable reception.   Kittl's "Jagd-Symphonie,"
which had been given in Paris with some success,
was performed in the presence of the composer,
who introduced himself as a humble amateur.
We also had one by the composer of the "Last
Judgment," the old Dessauer, as Friedrich Schnei-
der was often called.   Schubert's great C major
symphony* made such a powerful impression that
it was put down in the programme a second
time.   However, it had hardly begun when the
public took fright at a false alarm of fire, and

* Brought from Vienna by R. Schumann, and first performed, in MS.,
on 22nd March, 1839.—*Ed.*

fled. Afterwards it was played at the end of
the last concert, with much fire, and no alarm.
I also heard there, for the first and last time in
my life, a symphony by Vogler. Amongst the
overtures, Rietz's in A major especially deserves
mention, having become one of the best known
works of that composer. I happened to be with
Mendelssohn at the moment when he got the
score. He had known this excellent composition
at Düsseldorf, and was greatly delighted with
the successful alterations which had been made in
it, probably by his own advice. He soon found
a publisher for it, and was immensely excited
at being able to send the news to Rietz in his
musical solitude at Düsseldorf. At one of the
first concerts which I went to, a half improvised
performance of the four Leonora-Fidelio Overtures took place.* The first and second were in
the programme — the latter, then unpublished,
being given for the first time; it was received
with great enthusiasm, and encored, upon which
Mendelssohn gave the third, the greatest and best
known; and later in the concert, some instrumental solo having been omitted, he also gave
the fourth, the overture to "Fidelio," in E.
This wonderfully interesting conjunction of these

---

* It is well to preserve the date of this memorable musical event—
11th January, 1840.—*Ed.*

four masterpieces was all the more charming for
its not having been pre-arranged.

Amongst his choral works I must specially
mention the splendid Psalm, " When Israel out
of Egypt came," the first performance of which
took place on New Year's Day, 1840.   The
first movements of it are certainly among the
noblest of Mendelssohn's compositions, and will
always hold their own against the most important
things which our art has produced.   Neither the
novelty of the work nor the presence of the composer could add to its merit, but they certainly
heightened the impression, and it need not be said
that its reception was enthusiastic.   I also have
a very vivid remembrance of the performance of
a capital Finale from Cherubini's "Abencerrages,"
which Mendelssohn had taken great pains to get
from the directors of the Berlin Opera.

The solo vocal music at a great number of
the concerts was sustained by a charming young
Belgian lady, Mlle. Elise Meerti, and afterwards
by the well-known Sophie Schloss.   All manner
of Cavatinas out of unknown Italian Operas
(which the public of course enjoyed extremely)
had to be scored for the programmes, and to
our great delight these were so well done by
a very clever copyist as only to require
slight revision from Mendelssohn before perform-

ance. We often secretly chuckled over some of the bold orchestral effects which our poor copyist had successfully ventured upon at sixpence a sheet.

The instrumental solos were endless, and many of them capital. Mendelssohn played his D minor Concerto for the first time ; David and Ernst, Eckert (now Capellmeister at Berlin), Kalliwoda, and many others, contributed violin solos. One of the pianoforte performances I must mention, because of, or rather in spite of, my having a share in it. Felix and I were to play Mozart's E flat Concerto for two pianos, and had prepared the Cadenza for the first movement in the following manner. I was to begin extemporizing and make a pause on some chord of the seventh, Mendelssohn was then to continue and pause on another chord which we had fixed upon, and for the finish he had written a few pages for both instruments, now separately, now together, till the return of the Tutti. The thing succeeded perfectly, and the audience, few of whom could make out how we had managed it, applauded enthusiastically.

Besides these there were performances on the cello, the clarinet, the horn, the bassoon, the trombone, and even the musical glasses. The public were much more tolerant about such things at that time than now, when the piano-forte, violin, and cello have almost exclusive command of the concert-room.   No doubt this is of advantage to the programmes, but it is by no means so to the orchestras, as it entirely deprives the wind-instrument players of the opportunity of gaining a little extra honour and extra pay.   Thus it has come about that our much-vaunted improvement in executive music can only be called real with respect to the string instruments.   And the pre-ference given to the brass in modern music is likely to make the performance of works by the old masters more and more difficult.   But I am digressing, and must return to Leipsic.

The interest of the Quartet-Evenings, which Ferdinand David had carried on for some years past, was greatly heightened this winter by Men-delssohn's co-operation.   He often played at them, and his renderings of Mozart and Beethoven were incomparably beautiful.   He and I also occasion-ally played duets for four hands, and made a great sensation with Mozart's Variations in G. But what I remember most distinctly was his performance of Bach's Chromatic Fantasia ; it was quite overwhelming, and the applause was so great he was obliged to go back to the piano. He then improvised, combining in the cleverest way a theme of Bach's with his own well-known Song without Words in E (No. 1, Book 1)—thus uniting past and present into something new and difficult to describe. David was no less many-sided in *his* way ; in addition to the three great quartet writers he favoured us with Spohr, Onslow, and Mendelssohn, and also Schubert, then little known as a quartet composer. I must not forget to mention the fact that this winter he brought before the public the Chaconne of Bach, since so much played. Mendelssohn accompanied* *ad libitum* on the piano, and it was a great success. The public were also much delighted one evening to see Mendelssohn and Kalliwoda playing the violas in Spohr's double quartet and Mendelssohn's octet. Mendelssohn never touched a stringed instrument the whole year round, but if wanted he could do it—as he could most other things.

Nor must I forget, for the sake of that clever artist's friends, that during this season young Verhulst, who was in some measure a pupil of Mendelssohn's, earned his first spurs as conductor of the " Euterpe " concerts. At these he gave some very promising large choral works of his own composition.

---

* Mendelssohn afterwards published his accompaniment, and Schumann another, to this and other solos of Bach.—*Ed.*

This winter was remarkable for the appearances of some of the most brilliant players. First of all Ernst, then at the summit of his talent, and enchanting the whole world. Mendelssohn was very fond of him. Ernst told me one day, almost with emotion, how at the time of his concerts in the Königstädter Theatre at Berlin, he was very much pressed one morning in Mendelssohn's presence to put down his "Elégie" in the programme again, though he had already played it I don't know how many times. When Mendelssohn also began urging him to do it, Ernst answered, in fun : "If you will accompany me I will;" and Mendelssohn in fact made his appearance on the Königstädter stage, accompanied the "Elégie," and vanished. It was not only their beloved violins which united David and Ernst, but also the beloved game of whist. I certainly believe that neither of them ever played the violin so late into the night as they did whist. It was harmless enough, and good and bad jokes played just as great a part in it as the cards.

Towards the spring Liszt arrived in Leipsic fresh from his triumphs at Vienna and Prague, and revolutionized our quiet town. It will be remembered that in Paris he had excited Mendelssohn's highest admiration. At his first con-

cert, as he glided along the platform of the
orchestra to the piano, dressed in the most
elegant style, and as lithe and slender as a
tiger-cat, Mendelssohn said to me : "There's a
novel apparition, the virtuoso of the 19th century." I need hardly describe the impression made by his playing. When he played
Schubert's "Erlkönig" half the people stood
on their chairs. The Lucia fantasia turned
everybody's head. With some other pieces, however, he was less successful—for instance, with
Mendelssohn's D minor concerto, which had just
appeared, and which he could neither read at
sight nor find time to study with any care, so
that people thought that the composer played it
better himself. His performance of a part of
the Pastoral Symphony, in the same room where
it had so often been heard with all its orchestral
effects, also did not meet with general approval.
In the preface to his arrangement of the Beethoven Symphonies Liszt boldly declares that
every effect can be reproduced on the modern
piano. When Mendelssohn read this, he said :
"Well, if I could only hear the first eight bars
of Mozart's G minor Symphony, with that delicate
figure in the tenors, rendered on the piano as
it sounds in the orchestra,—I would believe it."

It may easily be imagined that Liszt was

fêted to the very utmost. Mendelssohn arranged
a grand soirée at the Gewandhaus to which
upwards of two hundred people were invited.
It was a half conversazione, half concert. I
had the honour of taking part in a performance
of Bach's concerto for three pianos. I myself
entertained Liszt at a rather solemn dinner on
the first floor of a fashionable hotel, and invited
all the heads of the musical societies in the place
to meet him. Some time afterwards, when we
were talking over these heroic social deeds of
ours, Mendelssohn was infinitely amused at hearing that my mere private fête, which had
included such a small number of people, cost me
much more than his grand demonstration. He
had such a childishly naïve and good-natured
way of laughing at anything of that sort, and
really was never so pleasant as when he could
be making fun of something or other.

At the last of the Gewandhaus Concerts* I
conducted my oratorio, the "Destruction of
Jerusalem." I had sent Mendelssohn a finished
sketch of it in the foregoing summer, and he at
once took the warmest interest in it; it was
certainly owing to his influence that, though the
score was not yet even written, the oratorio

---

* 2nd April, 1840.

should have been accepted for performance by the directors of the concerts. In the putting together of the words there was a great deal with which we were neither of us satisfied. One day he took the *libretto* home with him, and surprised me in the kindest way on Christmas Eve with a fresh and complete copy of it. I need not explain how useful his severe critical remarks were to my composition. One day when I thanked him he said : " I only show you what you would have found out for your-self in a few months." The oratorio had a very warm reception ; but what pleased me most was Mendelssohn's entire satisfaction. He sat amongst the audience with Cécile, and told me what pleasure he had felt not only in my music but also in the correct judgment of his wife, who had always picked out the best things. He also admitted that the work had a very peculiar colouring, and I only refer to this now because it has sometimes been spoken of as an imitation of the " Elijah," which was not completed till six years later.

In the course of that winter Mendelssohn published a number of works, and amongst others his D minor trio.* He went on correcting

---

* Op. 49.

and altering it up to the last minute, and many of the plates had to be engraved over again. He also composed a good many new things. But what occupied him most of all was the " Hymn of Praise " (Lobgesang) which he had undertaken to compose for the commemoration of the discovery of printing, in June 1840. How he managed to work in the midst of so many distractions it would be difficult to imagine but for his wonderful mental equanimity. In general he was completely master of his powers, though I do not mean to say that he could or would have composed at any moment—but he certainly often did so when one would least have expected it. " When I go into a painter's studio," he once said to me, " I am often envious. It must be too nice to live all day entirely for one's work, as they do. But our independent way of spending our time has a great charm about it too." Of this independence he made the greatest use, and probably never spent his time alike two days running. One afternoon I found him particularly cheerful, and he said to me : " I have had such a satisfactory morning : I have been playing a great deal, all sorts of people's music, and yours too, and also composing and writing. I mean to do this every day now ! " And yet he hardly managed it a second time. His correspondence really took up most of his time, and the number of letters he must have written is incredible. But it was a pleasure to him to be in such general requisition, and he never complained of it. Everything he did he strove to do in the most perfect manner possible, down to the smallest details, and it was the same with his correspondence. It was delightful to see the care and evident satisfaction with which he would fold and seal his letters. Anyhow, he could always feel sure of their giving pleasure. Whatever hard work he had before him it never prevented him from occupying himself with something else up to the last minute. How often, when I called for him to go to a concert where he had to play and conduct, I would find him in full dress, sitting quietly at the writing-table! It was just because he felt so secure in all that he did.

"How would you translate this?" he asked me one evening, and then read me a line out of one of Dante's Sonnets. His uncle Joseph (the eldest son of Moses Mendelssohn, who dedicated his "Morgenstunden" to him), a very highly-gifted man, and devoted to his latest years to study and self-culture, had sent him several of Dante's Sonnets from the "Vita Nuova," begging him to translate them for him in the form of the original.

The nephew set to work with feverish eagerness; and, as far as I could judge, succeeded admirably. But after all he got more vexation than pleasure from it, for the old gentleman, with an uncle's want of consideration, had meanwhile made use of some other version, and Felix did not even get a word of thanks, whereat he greatly complained. I take this opportunity of saying that I feel sure that Felix must have written a considerable number of lyrical poems, though I do not know if he told his friends of it. If I am right, we may surely hope that some future time may bring them to light. They would certainly not be without merit.

Another partly literary work which occupied my friend for some time was an address to the King of Saxony. A sum of 20,000 thalers had been bequeathed to the king by a Leipsic gentleman, with the request that it should be devoted to some artistic purpose. In conjunction with Von Falkenstein, then "Kreis-director," and now Minister, Mendelssohn drew up the plan for the organisation of a Conservatorium, to which he added an entreaty that the king would devote the money in question to the foundation of the institution. It is well known that the Leipsic Conservatorium was opened in the year 1843, that Mendelssohn laboured enthusiastically for it,

and that this school contributed greatly to the
progress of musical life in Leipsic. It was
equally Mendelssohn's doing that Hauptmann
and Moscheles were appointed to posts there.

One evening I found Felix deep in the Bible.
"Listen," he said; and then he read to me, in
a gentle and agitated voice, the passage from the
First Book of Kings, beginning with the words,
"And behold, the Lord passed by." "Would
not that be splendid for an oratorio?" he
exclaimed—and it did become part of the
"Elijah."

In the midst of the manifold occupations and
social meetings in which he gladly took part, and
which he graced by his talent and brilliant conversation, there would come days of exhaustion,
even of depression. At such times, visits from
his friends, foremost among whom were David
and Dr. Schleinitz, would always do him good.
Sometimes he would amuse himself with doing
little water-colour sketches—or he would read
some poem of Goethe's, such as "Hermann and
Dorothea" or "Iphigenie." The first of these he
was especially fond of, and he would go into
raptures over the deep feeling which penetrates
the most insignificant things in that wonderful
work. He said one day that the line,

Und es lobte darauf der Apotheker den Knaster,

was enough to bring tears into one's eyes. He would also get out Jean Paul sometimes, and revel in his humour; one evening he read aloud to me out of Siebenkäs for at least an hour. But sleep was always his best resource. Several times I found him lying on the sofa before dinner, ready dressed, having been asleep for hours, after which he would awake with a capital appetite. A quarter of an hour after he would say with the air of a spoiled child, "I am still quite tired;" would lie down again, saying how delicious it was, stretch himself out, and in a few minutes be fast asleep again. "He can go on in that way for two days," Cécile said to me, "and then he is fresher than ever." Nature supplied him with the best cure—but unhappily it could not remain so always.

For his birthday we arranged a joke with which he was immensely delighted. The first idea of it arose from the fact that his wife and her sister and myself were of the same nation, the free town of Frankfort being our common native place. I wrote a little piece, or rather a couple of scenes, in Frankfort dialect, giving myself the part of the now typical "Hampelmann."* Ma-

---

* "Hampelmann" is the name of the typical Frankfort burgher, a favourite character in farces.—*Ed.*

dame Mendelssohn was to represent my wife, and her sister my daughter. The story was somewhat slight, and ran as follows :—Fräulein Hampelmann is a very passionate lover of music, and in the first scene expresses a great wish to have pianoforte lessons from the celebrated Mendelssohn at Leipsic. After much discussion the papa is gained over, and the family prepare for the journey. The second scene opened in Mendelssohn's study, where he was represented by David with inimitable drollery. The costume was true to life, being the very coat which Mendelssohn wore at home, and David managed in all sorts of delightful ways to caricature our friend's movements and manner of speaking. The Hampelmann family are introduced to him, and very politely received. After some conversation Fräulein Hampelmann is made to play, and then Mendelssohn is at last induced to improvise, and this David did in the funniest way, imitating Mendelssohn in his movements more than in his thoughts. Finally this good-natured, but not very artistic family, is sent home again in the most civil manner possible. I had made the Hampelmann ladies, in their excessively limited knowledge of musical matters, say all manner of malicious things, which were taken as pleasantly as they were harmlessly meant.

When our life had become a little quieter
so that we often spent the evenings at home,
Mendelssohn proposed that we should improvise
on given poems. We read and played in turns,
each declaiming for the other, and found it a
most amusing and exciting pastime. Heaven
only knows how many poems of Schiller, Goethe,
and Uhland had to serve us for musical illus-
trations. After one of my improvisations Mendelssohn said to me, " I can't imagine how you
can ever for a moment feel any doubt about
your musical gifts ; " and these words often
afterwards in sad moments rang with consolation
in my ears. During my subsequent stay in
Dresden I had the opportunity of continuing
these improvisations with my friend Edward
Devrient, who perhaps declaimed better than
anyone else, certainly more musically. In this
way we were able to give great pleasure, and
as an amusing social diversion, I have often,
even up to the present time, carried on this
game with some friend or other, and it always
recalls the happy times in which we first began it.

We had many serious conversations together
that winter, and I very much regret that I did
not note down some of my friend's sayings. But
when one is living in affluence one does not
readily think of putting by. A few things which

I happen to remember may find room here.   After
the performance of a most prosaic symphony,
which met with a very cold reception, he said
to me, "We have successfully conquered the
Philistines now, but it remains to be seen whether our Art will not be still more threatened
from the opposite side."   Once when I was speaking of the happiness that lay in the conviction
of so many people whom one highly esteemed
being kindly disposed towards one, he grew very
excited upon the subject, and said, "It is certainly the best thing that one has.   When I am
thoroughly dissatisfied with myself, I think of
such and such a person who has shown himself
a friend to me, and say to myself, 'You can't
be in such a bad way, after all, if such men
are fond of you.'"   One day, speaking of his
adherents and his opponents, he said that he
could perfectly understand that certain musicians
who took up the very strict line considered him
half a deserter, because many of those of his
compositions which met with most favour must
appear to them frivolous compared to former
ones, and therefore they might say he had for-
saken his better style.

With his earnest character, it was especially
disagreeable to him when people treated serious
things with exaggeration.   "I had a visit from

a Belgian author this morning," he told me,
a few hours later; "the man really has an
astounding flow of talk, and said several good
things. But when he was gone, and I began
to think it over, I found that it might have been
expressed much better in the very simplest way :
therefore why use such big words? why want
to appear so deep?" It is this simplicity, always
exemplified in his works, which makes them
appear shallow to those people who take bom-
bastic nonsense for depth. There is no shallow-
ness to be found in Mendelssohn's works, but
rather in those which are too shallow to contain
the beauty of simplicity.

Once at dinner, when we were talking about
Beaumarchais' comedies, which he greatly admired, he said, " One really ought to have
Beaumarchais ;" so I got it for him and wrote
inside it, " One really ought to have Beaumarchais (Mendelssohn's table talk)."

One peculiarity of his, which I have already
alluded to, was his way of suddenly jumping to
something very comic or very serious in the
midst of a quiet conversation. One afternoon
when we were lounging about in the prome-
nades, he turned upon me all at once with the
question : " Do you believe in the progress of
humanity ? " " How, in what way do you

mean ? " I said, with some surprise. " Well," he answered, " I don't speak of machines, and railways, and all those things, but I ask if you think that mankind becomes better and more remarkable as time goes on ? " I do not now remember what conclusion we came to.

It was always from the way in which he had been taught that he drew his reasons for everything which he did, or did not do. Thus in the scores of his choruses he always used the C clef, and kept the alto part also in the soprano clef. This rather puzzled me, and I once reproached him for the inconsistency of such a proceeding, upon which he answered, " You are perfectly right, but it is not my fault. It was Zelter's way, and I accustomed myself to it from the very first." His lovely musical handwriting he said he owed to his friend Edward Rietz the violin-player, who died young, and was the elder brother of Julius Rietz, the Capellmeister.

He sometimes talked to me about his studies with Zelter, and of the peripatetic way in which they were usually carried on in the garden behind his father's house. What he told me of them confirmed me in the opinion which Marx expressed when he said that " when Zelter became Mendelssohn's master, he merely put the fish

N

into the water, and let it swim away as it liked."
With all his love for his old teacher, the remembrance of the following fact always made him
angry. Some years before Felix's birth, his
father, who was a friend of Zelter's, gave the
latter a great quantity of Bach's Cantatas in the
original manuscripts; and when Felix became his
pupil, Zelter used sometimes to take him to the
closet where these treasures were stored up, and
show them to him, saying, "There they are; just
think of all that is hidden there!" But poor
Felix, though he thirsted for these costly treasures, was never once allowed to look inside
them, and taste them. They would certainly
have been better cared for in Mendelssohn's
hands than in Zelter's.

Mendelssohn was very fond of repeating a
funny expression or word over and over again
till it became a joke. As in former years he
had amused himself with calling me "Old
Drama," so now during this winter, for a long
time he always addressed me with the words,
"Hail, Zedckiah!" out of one of my choruses
in the "Destruction of Jerusalem." Or else it
would be a passage out of some pianoforte piece
which he liked, and which he would always be
bringing up again, and playing to me when it
was furthest from my thoughts.

I also have pleasant recollections of the walks which we· often took with David, on clear, cold days, far out into the Rosenthal. We used to stop at one of the cafés there, and Mendelssohn would indulge in his latest, but as I believe, very passing, passion for billiards. Whether he was as clever at that as at everything else I could not judge, for though I lived many years in the land of billiards, I knew nothing of the game.

It may seem strange that I should not have mentioned Schumann, especially as Mendelssohn thought so highly of him, but at that time he lived in greater retirement than usual, and hardly ever left his room. His newspaper, his songs, but above all his approaching marriage with Clara Wieck, completely occupied him; his bride, already celebrated, did not often come to Leipsic that winter, but a few years afterwards at Dresden I enjoyed a great deal of pleasant and intimate intercourse with the famous pair.

Everyone knows how happy Mendelssohn was at home. His beautiful, gentle, sensible wife spread a charm over the whole household, and reminded one of a Rafael Madonna. Little Carl, the eldest child, amused us intensely with his first attempts at speaking. Cécile's family, charming people, were in and out all day, and the whole

atmosphere was a sort of rivalry of amiability
and affection,—it was a period of happiness which
falls to the share of but few mortals. We
laughed much when Cécile told us how, as she
came out of a concert at the Gewandhaus, she
had heard two women talking about her and
pitying her because "her husband was so cruel,
inhuman, and barbarous to her !"

All this time, though I was very much occupied with my work, and looking forward with
anxiety to the first performance of the oratorio,
I could feel and enjoy to the utmost the happiness which Mendelssohn's affection and esteem
imparted to me. And at last, when my labours
were crowned by an entirely unbiassed success,
the concluding days of my stay in Leipsic became
some of the happiest in my life. On the 2nd of
April, 1840, the "Destruction of Jerusalem" was
performed for the first time at a concert given
at the Gewandhaus for the benefit of the poor.
The chorus and orchestra were capital ; Frau Livia
Frege, whose lovely and expressive singing can
never be forgotten by any who had the good
fortune to hear her, Fräulein Sophie Schloss, with
her fine sympathetic voice, the clever tenor,
Schmidt, and a very cultivated amateur baritone,
undertook the solos. The audience was enthusiastic, and next morning my excellent publisher,

Kistner, secured the work as his property—what more could I desire? I returned full of gratitude to my native town, which I had left with such a sad heart, and from thence went on to Italy, where my bride awaited me.

CHAPTER VII.

My chief authority for this period is my journal, which, though short enough, I kept very regularly. Having spent the first winter after my marriage in Rome, I returned to Frankfort with my young wife in the summer of 1842, and was most kindly welcomed by my numerous friends, amongst whom I may reckon those connected with Mendelssohn by his wife. Felix came to Frankfort with his family in September, and stayed a fortnight. My wife had cultivated her beautiful soprano voice with great care in Italy, and for some months was very successful on the stage. Mendelssohn took the greatest interest in her musical gifts, and his short visit that autumn was like a musical spring to us. He generally spent half the day at our house, and we used to meet him and his wife at parties nearly every evening. I had filled a thick blue music-book with music of all sorts, German and

Italian psalms, airs and romances, which I had composed for my wife, and all of these Mendelssohn insisted on hearing; in fact, he never came to see us without asking for the blue book. Carl Müller, a clever painter, whose acquaintance we had made in Rome, happening to be in Frankfort just at this time, promised to do us a pencil sketch of Mendelssohn if we could only get him to sit. At my wife's request he consented to put himself into the painter's hands, on condition that she would sing to him during the time. Sixteen songs of various lengths completed the sitting, and this sketch, with his autograph and the date of the 15th September, 1842, is one of our greatest treasures.*

A few days before his departure he wrote in my wife's album a setting of the Volkslied,

"Es weiss und räth es doch Keiner,
Wie mir so wohl ist, so wohl"—

and painted underneath it a miniature map of Germany, to impress her new country on her mind. Next to the map he drew a pair of yellow kid gloves, as a sign of his endeavour to attain the height of elegance. After his return to Leipsic he continued his gallant behaviour by

---

* See the Frontispiece of this Volume.

writing her an Italian letter, which I shall give in its proper place.

At that time he chiefly played to me the choruses from his " Antigone." He delighted to recall the energetic way in which he had pushed forward and fixed the performance, in opposition to Tieck's hesitation and doubt; and as usual in such cases gave me amusing and graphic accounts of his little devices for getting round the famous old poet; he seemed to enjoy all this almost more than the beautiful work itself, which had taken him only just over a fortnight to compose. He had completed his great A minor symphony * in the course of the summer, and was at work on a four-hand arrangement of it for the pianoforte, which he made haste to finish on my account. During his stay we had invited our Frankfort acquaintances for the first time to a musical Matinée; Felix completed the arrangement the evening before, and we began our music with this glorious work.

As usual Mendelssohn's time was always entirely taken up in some way or other with music. Charles Halle, who has since gained such a high artistic position in England, came to

* The " Scotch Symphony." The Autograph score is dated "20th January, 1842."—*Ed.*

Frankfort with his charming wife during that fortnight. Being totally unknown there, the prospects of a concert which he intended giving were perhaps not so brilliant as his great talent deserved. So I persuaded Mendelssohn to help us, and we played Bach's Triple Concerto; in consequence the room was crowded, everyone wanted to see Mendelssohn at the piano, and Halle's success was complete.

Another day he played on the organ at St. Catherine's church, and this, as may be imagined, attracted a great number of musical people. But I confess that even Mendelssohn's famous talent, like that of many other eminent organists, left me quite cold, though I am far from attributing this to any want in their playing. I find it immensely interesting to stand by an organist and watch the motions of his hands and feet whilst I follow on the music. But the excessive resonance in churches makes it more pain than pleasure to me to listen from below to any of those wonderful creations, with their manifold intricacies and brilliant passages. When I saw near me so many cultivated musical people in the greatest delight, I was obliged to admit that the fault must lie in my imperfect musical organisation. Or did they only show their delight because it was the correct thing to do? That

also is possible. As an accompaniment to con-
gregational singing, or for strengthening the
harmony in oratorio choruses, the organ is indispensable, sublime, unique. But as a solo instrument I can only enjoy it when the greatest
care is taken both in the choice and performance
of such pieces as lie completely within its pro-
vince. To make use of the organ for secular
music is to misuse it; but many even of the
great works written expressly for it, though
suitable in feeling, are not effective in a church.
The organ is a queen who should only show
herself when surrounded by her choicest state.

Mendelssohn was immensely excited whenever
he played the organ, and indeed, even for musical
organisations less highly developed than his, it
must be most intoxicating to revel in that ocean
of sound. Still, there is a gulf between making
music and listening to it.

He also accompanied us to the opera a few
times, and I may here recall a gay remark of his
as we were listening to a performance of the
" Favorita" for the first time. In the opening
scene, if I am not mistaken, there is a chorus of
monks, which begins with an ascending scale,
accompanied by the orchestra in rather an old-
fashioned style. "Now they will sing the
descending scale," said Felix; and he was right.

The young singers of Frankfort were determined again to do honour to the famous composer,
and a great *fête* was given at the " Sandhof," with
part songs, tableaux vivants, toasts, speeches, and
the like.   It was very pretty, though it had none
of the poetry of the one which Mendelssohn so
charmingly describes in a letter to his mother,
3rd July, 1839.*   I was in Italy at that time,
and was only represented by some of my songs
which were sung.   But I cannot resist going
back a few years, and quoting a letter from
one of the ladies who helped to arrange the *fête,*
because it gives such a vivid picture of the chief
figure :—

" Everything went off beautifully, and it was
just as if God had given His blessing to the
whole affair.   Mendelssohn seems not to have
been able to wait till the time fixed, for he and
his lovely young wife arrived much too early.
But he adapted himself to the situation with
the greatest good humour, and watched the preparations for his reception with infinite delight.
I have never seen such a perfectly happy being
as he was when he heard his quartets sung for
the first time in the wood.   His whole face
beamed, his eyes literally sparkled with pleasure,

See also *ante,* page 73.

and he was so excited that he actually danced
about on one leg, calling out after each song,
'Again, again, please, once more!' We had to
do the 'Lark's Song' three times running with
all the repeats."

It was in consequence of this *fête* that he
dedicated the first book of his "Part-songs for
the Open Air" to Dr. Spiess and Herr Martin,
two very musical gentlemen who had greatly
helped in the preparation of the party.

But to return to 1842. On the 25th Mendelssohn went to Leipsic, and then to Berlin.
It was only twenty years afterwards that I
learned from the published collection of some of
his letters in 1863 what a truly friendly action
he had done for me during that very time.
Amongst these letters I discovered one to Simrock, the publisher in Bonn, in favour of someone whom the editors of the letters discreetly
designate as "X." There was no doubt about
my being this unknown quantity; and having
revealed the secret, I cannot resist reprinting the
letter again, for it displays such a wonderful amount
of tender consideration and loving sympathy. It
is dated Frankfort, the 21st September :—

DEAR MR. SIMROCK,—I write to you to-day
about a matter in which I must count on your

entire discretion and profound secresy; your kindness towards me I know too well from experience to doubt the fulfilment of my wish, and I put the matter before you fully relying on your silence. I heard quite by chance, during my stay here, that my friend and fellow-artist, Mr. F. Hiller, had written to you about the publication of some new works, but as yet had received no answer. I wish very much, in the interest of art as well as in that of my friend, that your answer may be favourable; and as I fancy that my opinion may have some weight with you, it occurred to me to write to you about it, and beg you, if you possibly could, to make the German public acquainted with some of my friend's works. My reason for begging you to keep the matter secret from *everybody* and under *all circumstances,* is that I am certain that Mr. Hiller would be frantic if he had the remotest idea of my having taken such a step. I know that nothing would be more unbearable to him than not to stand altogether on his own feet, and therefore he must *never* know anything about this letter. But, on the other hand, it is a duty and obligation which one artist owes to another to help him as much as possible over difficulties and disagreeables, and to give him every assistance towards the attainment of the

efforts, provided they are noble and the cause a
good one.   And certainly this is true in the
very highest degree, both of his efforts and his
cause.   That is why I wanted to beg you to
publish some of his compositions, and above all,
if possible, to enter into some sort of agreement
with him.   I know perfectly well that the
German publishers have not done any very
brilliant business (as it is called) with most of
his works as yet, and I cannot ensure its being
different now ; but that this *deserves* to be
otherwise I feel no doubt whatever, and this is
my reason, and my only reason, for making you
this request.   Were it not so, however great a
friend he might be of mine, I would not ask it.

But just because the only consideration which
ought reasonably to be entertained is that of
intrinsic worth, and because it is the only one
which *ought* to insure success if everything were
carried on fairly in this world, and because it is
too annoying to hear the old story repeated for
ever of the deserving and clever artists who at
first have the greatest difficulty in getting their
music brought out and made known, and afterwards are made a fuss about by everybody when
one of their works happens to make a hit and
gains the ear of the public—though, after all,
neither the pleasure nor the fuss can make up

for their former troubles—just because of all this
I want you to act differently, and to believe
more in real work than in chance success. It
must be put a stop to some day, and the only
question in such cases is how soon, and after
how many disagreeables; and that is just the
point where a publisher may be of so much
value and importance to an artist. Universal
applause brings them all to the front, of course;
but I feel that you would be just the man to
reform this state of things, and bring about one
which should be at once ideal, practical, and
just. Pray forgive my boldness, and if possible
fulfil my request. As far as I understand, a
large remuneration is of no consequence; but it is
of the greatest importance that you should write
in a friendly and artistic tone, that the works
should be published and well diffused, and finally,
if you are willing and able to carry out the
matter, that my share in it, my name, and my
request, be kept *completely secret*. How happy
it would make me if I were shortly to hear from
him that you had written, and made him a kind
offer to publish some of his new songs and
pianoforte pieces! After all, perhaps you will
only say " What does this idle composer and
still more idle correspondent mean?" But I certainly have improved in my correspondence, as

you may see from this, and in the other matter
I mean to improve very shortly, and shall assail
you with music-paper (as soon as it is well filled),
and beg you, in my own name, what I have
begged so earnestly and fervently for my friend.

Always yours faithfully,

FELIX MENDELSSOHN BARTHOLDY.

The following extract from a subsequent letter
of his from Berlin to Simrock also deserves a
place here :—

If ever I was agreeably surprised by a letter,
I was so by yours which I received here yesterday.
The kind and quick fulfilment of my wish, and
the large sum which you sent me for my " Songs
without Words "—I really do not know how to
thank you enough, or express the great pleasure
you have given me ; I must confess I had hardly
expected so hearty and complete a response as
your immediate reply to my letter, and am now
doubly glad that I took a step from which, even
as I wrote, I was very nearly withheld by false
shame, and by that fatal worldly-wise maxim
about not meddling with other people's affairs.
I feel that your conduct, as exemplified in your
yesterday's letter, only confirms me afresh in

what I believe to be good and right, so I shall hang up the much-vaunted worldly wisdom on a nail,* and go straight ahead, following my own first impulses and feelings. Even if I fail a hundred times, one *such* success is ample amends.

We composers, though possibly more inclined than other artists to devour each other (which lies in the nature of things), are still not so bad but what we often do one another such services as Mendelssohn did me by means of this letter. But this was done without any encouragement, quite secretly, without the possibility of receiving any thanks, much less a future return, even without the satisfaction of having patronised me. Perhaps it is just the secrecy of the service rendered which makes it a thing so rarely heard of. But nobody who has not made the experience can imagine the overpowering, elevating feeling it gives one to hear of such a deed long after the death of a friend.

The following letters I received soon afterwards from Berlin and Leipsic :—

BERLIN, 8*th October*, 1842.

DEAR FERDINAND, — We arrived here quite safe and well, but still it seems to me as if it

---

* An expression of his father's. See the published Letter Jan. 30, 1836.—*Ed.*

O

were already centuries since I left the " Fahrthor,"
and as if Berlin were a thousand miles from
Frankfort.   There's nothing worse than travelling
north in the autumn; for the yellow leaves, and
the bare trees, and cold blasts, and hot stoves,
seem to come upon one quicker and quicker till
one is right in the midst of them, and then one
sees the court carriages all out, and eats sour
grapes and bad nuts, and wastes a deal of
breath in grumbling over them, and at the same
time bores oneself and everybody else but——
Oh dear, I am already falling back into the old
Berlin strain!   But why *is* everything better in
the south ?   The people, the fruit, the weather,
the country, and everything ?   Your wife won't
hear of its being so—but that doesn't alter it.
At Leipsic I was told that there had been a
musical morning-soiree at Ferdinand Hiller's last
Sunday, with Herwegh and other notabilities.
And then, as I said before, it did seem to me
no end of a time since I left the " Rothmännche,"* though it was only three hours
before the said morning-soiree ; but I was already
at Langensebold whilst the " Rothmännche " was
resounding with good fine music.

This is really a business letter, though you

---

* The name of the house we then lived in at Frankfort.

may not think so. I was at S.'s yesterday
about your message. He says he will have your
songs engraved, and then, when he gets your
answer he will be able to publish them in six
weeks, with a German translation, which we both
thought desirable; if you are satisfied with the
whole arrangement, he begs that you will fix
the day of publication for him and for Ricordi.
He made difficulties about engraving the Cello
Sonata, because he has just now got to engrave
the whole of Halevy's "Queen of Cyprus," besides
all sorts of arrangements and potpourris of it,
and could not publish any large work at the
same time; however, if you like, he will write
to Ricordi, and order a hundred copies from
him, and get him to put the name of his (S.'s)
firm on the title-page, and then he will see that
it gets known in Germany. I could not exactly
make out what particular advantage this would
be to you, but as he insisted, I was at last
obliged to promise that I would write to you,
and so I do it. If I have done wrong, send me
your "Hattischerif," but without the bow-string.
S. is the only publisher here (Z. is the essence
of Berlin Philistinism bottled, and sprinkled
over a music-shop), so he does what he likes,
and you have to cringe if you want to get
anything published in Berlin. The day before

yesterday they gave Rossini's "William Tell" *as a new opera*, for the first time, to celebrate the grand wedding, &c. (what should I know about it?) They cut it down to three acts, and announced it "as arranged by the composer for the stage in Paris." Since then it has been the talk all over Berlin every day, whether or not it is Rossini's true vocation to be a composer— that is to say, whether he has been able to rise to the level of dramatic music, and possesses the inspiration for it—whether, in fact, it was justifiable to choose such a subject, Schiller's tragedy being certainly a far more perfect work of art than this opera—whether meanwhile, &c., &c. (Oh dear! how good the dinners at the "Mainlust" are!) Certainly the Philistinism of all the rest of Germany put together is nothing compared to this spiritual "Michel," this immortal Nicolai,* who blooms and blossoms in all discussions on art, and peeps out of every Berlin form of speech. But now I am tired of this dry tone, and must talk to your wife in Italian.

ILLUSTRISSIMA SIGNORA!—S'io avessi voluto aspettare la esecuzione della sua promessa, voglio

---

* "Michel" is the German "John Bull." Nicolai was rendered "immortal" by a work on Italy, solely remarkable for the wholesale way in which he abuses that country.—*Ed.*

dire il ricevimento d'une lettera Italiana scritta
da lei, io avessi potuto aspettare lungo tempo.
Per questa raggione debbo fra il comminciamento e domandarla come sta la vostra salute?
Spero che il rhumo del quale Lei soffriva allora
è partito lungo tempo fà, e che la sua voce è
da capo chiara e bella come sopra. Il paese quì
non mi piace a fatto; vado frà dubbio e sospiri,
navigando in un mar di pene, senza ramie e senza
vele. Vorrei aver il coraggio di dir al fine:
così sì fà; ma la mia indecisione è sempre più
forte di me.   Qualche volta vorrei sentirla cantare soltanto un quarto d'ora; darei in cambio
tutte le opere del Teatro Reale, dove si ascolta
un canto pessimo. Adesso voglio finire. La
mia moglie gli fà cento complimenti e pregandola
di scusare gli sbagli che forse si troveranno nel
mio stilo italiano, sono sempre con molta considerazione il suo umilissimo,

FELICE MENDELSSONIO BARTHOLDI.

The fact is that I am a little ashamed of these
last lines, on reading them over this evening;
but as I had to write to you directly, and in
the hurry of my arrival have no time for another
letter, you must excuse the bad old jokes, and
remain my true old friends. Good-bye for to-day.

Always your FELIX M.

LEIPSIC, 19*th January*, 1843.

MY DEAR GOOD FERDINAND. — When your
letter of the 16th of November arrived (it wàs
the best and nicest that I have ever had from
you, and not one has ever given me so much
pleasure, or touched me much more), I determined at once to write to you the next day,
and at the same time to thank your wife for
her affectionate lines. I put it off a few days—
and now what a terrible gulf there is between
that time and this!* I have to thank you for
a second letter since then, another proof of
your true friendship and kindness to me.
Till now I could not think of letter-writing,
or I should have thanked you at once,
and have already done so many times in my
heart. But at first I could do nothing, at
most read a few pages or so, and it was only
some weeks afterwards, when I could occupy
myself with any routine musical work, or with
writing music, that I began to feel a little better
—but letters were not to be thought of, and the
least conversation with my most intimate friends
would bring back the dull, confused feeling in
my head, a sort of stunned sensation, together
with the sorrow. I have had to conquer it these

---

* He had lost his mother on the 12th of December.

last three days, the mass of business letters had
accumulated to such an enormous degree; and
having once begun writing I felt that I must at
least send you a few words of greeting and
thanks; it won't be much more to-day. You
know my feelings towards you and yours and the
deep interest I take in your welfare; let me hear
of it soon and often, for it always cheers me
and gives me pleasure. Thank God, my wife
and children are well, and I really ought never
to do anything but thank Heaven on my knees
for such happiness. When I am alone with them
drawing windmills for the children, putting the
oboes and violas into the score, or correcting tiresome proof-sheets, I sometimes feel quite cheerful
and happy again; but when I begin to think of
other things, or have to see people, and look after
the rehearsals or concerts which I have to go on
conducting directly afterwards, it is as bad as
ever. So I am not at home for anybody all day,
except between three and four, and sit in my
little study, which I have now arranged, and
where I am most comfortable; it is the old
nursery, which you will remember, just opposite
the front door, with a beautiful view over mea-
dows and fields towards the sunset. Schumann
and David we see sometimes, A. hardly ever,
for he really only lives and breathes for the

Subscription Concerts, and I am very little good there just now—and so the days slip on. May yours be all the brighter and happier! I hear of your giving great Charity Concerts, and also that your new work is soon to be performed. I hope you will tell me about it, and confirm the good news.

You ask for details of my present position. The King of Prussia has allowed me to return here, and stay till he wants me in Berlin; in that case I have promised to go back. I have since written to him, that until I am personally established in Berlin I wish to give up half my salary, and meantime will carry out all his instructions here. Thereupon he wrote to me here that he was satisfied with this; he has also given me a new title, but otherwise there has been no change of any importance. In a word I am only awaiting here what I was at first to have awaited in Berlin, namely, that I should be indispensably needed there. I still doubt whether that will ever be the case, and hope (more than ever now, as you may imagine) that the King of Prussia will allow the present state of things to continue. What made me specially cling to Berlin, what in fact produced that consultation, or rather combination, no longer exists now.

The interest of that bequest, which I petitioned for more than three years ago for a school of music, has at last been granted, and now the official announcements will appear in the newspapers. I shall have to go to the Gewandhaus three or four times a week and talk about 6-4 chords in the small hall there. I am quite willing to do this for love of the cause, because I believe it to be a good cause.

How thankful I am to you for counting me amongst those with whom you like to be, and how heartily I respond to all you say about it. Indeed, it could not be so with one, unless the other felt exactly the same. We think we shall not travel this year, but probably spend the summer here or at Dresden. Is there any hope of our seeing you here? You once spoke of it. Best and kindest remembrances to your wife from me and mine; thank her for her sympathy, and beg her to keep us a place in her heart, and think of us sometimes, as we do daily with fond affection of you both, in good and evil times.

Your FELIX M. B.

LEIPSIC, *March 3rd,* 1843.

DEAR FERDINAND,—Best thanks for your dear, good, kind, long letter, which gave me great pleasure; I was especially glad of what you say

about your Opera, and your own satisfaction with
it, and its conclusion; *you* feel this now that
your work is done, whilst others would only feel
it on the day of performance, after receiving
laurel wreaths and poems, and such like; but
really the satisfaction can only be true and genuine
when one's work is finished. I am quite delighted
with all that you say about it, and I have no
doubt whatever that a work written in such a
spirit, and from the depths of your soul, cannot
fail to make an impression on your countrymen.

But it will not only meet with success, it
will deserve it—which in these days is saying
ten thousand times more. How I look forward
to it! Pray don't dream of letting the first performance be anywhere but in Frankfort; it would
be the greatest mistake. You know how much
importance I attach to one's native country; in
your present circumstances I attach it also to
your native town; they are fond of you there,
they know all about you, and have to make
amends for former slights in their behaviour
towards you; and little as I should like to enforce
this for the sake of making a bad thing pass for
good, so much the more would I do it to ensure
success for a good thing. Besides, *all* the theatres
in Germany are at present in a bad state, so do
not let yourself be deterred by any defect in

your Frankfort theatre; rather try and improve it, and all the others as well by degrees.

How can you wonder at N.'s success? They put all that into the newspapers themselves; and you who read them don't know what to think of it all, whilst I, meantime, am much better off, for I have become such a *Septem-briseur* against all newspapers that I believe nothing, absolutely nothing, except what I see with my eyes on the music-paper, or hear with my ears. Unfortunately it is somewhat the same thing with Wagner; I am afraid that a great deal becomes exaggerated in that quarter; and just those musicians whom I know to be conscientious people, increase my fear not a little. Still I have not yet heard any connected things out of his operas, and I always think that they must be better than people say. Talent he has most certainly, and I was delighted that he got that place, though even that made him enemies enough in the course of those few weeks, as I will tell you when we meet and go for a walk together at sunset.

Your question about your oratorio at Berlin you must explain to me more clearly; what do you mean by "being able to give a performance?" Do you want to give a concert on purpose, or do you merely want to give it a hearing at the Sing-Akademie or elsewhere? The subscription concerts here begin on the 1st of October; there is no regular musical season in Berlin before the middle of September; so that if you come, as you say, towards the end of August and spend a few quiet weeks with us, here or in Dresden, it would then be the regular concert season. Now do carry this out, and fulfil these fine plans and promises as soon as the summer comes on.

You remind me to take a good singing-master for our Music School. Please tell me if there is one to be found in all Germany. Meantime I have had hard work to stop them from altogether doing away with the teaching of singing, which is almost more necessary than anything else. Thirty-four pupils have sent in their names, and the school is to be opened in the middle of April. Schumann will teach the piano, and so shall I.

Next Thursday, as I hear, is the hundredth anniversary of the foundation of the Leipsic Subscription Concerts, and the orchestra is to have a supper. My symphony is out, and to be had since yesterday; Guhr did not say anything definite about it, or I should have sent it to him sooner. I hunted out that Scena for Mdlle. Schloss, for her Benefit Concert, wrote a new

Allegro to it, and so helped to make a full room. Otherwise it has little merit. I have written the Walpurgis Night all over again from A to Z; in fact, it is altogether a different thing now, and a hundred times better. But I am still in doubt about having it engraved. Many remembrances to your wife from me and mine. Don't forget your FELIX.

LEIPSIC, March 25th, 1843.

MY DEAR FERDINAND,—If it be one of the evils of separation that good moods pass away before any answer can be made to them, it is one of its good points that bad moods also pass away before they can be answered. I hope this is so with your letter of to-day, and shall therefore not inquire much into your depression, but firmly believe that it has already gone by, and that you are as contented with yourself, with your work, and consequently with everything else, as I always wish you to be, and as you were in your first letter. Besides, if that state of cheerful contentment with himself and his works becomes habitual to a man, I look upon him as a regular Philistine, and believe that he will never do anything decent all his life long, so I don't complain of your desponding remarks.

And when you declare that you have a real
liking for any musical sphere of action, you
meet with a hearty response from me and from
all your friends and all musicians; and your
insane misgivings about the "doubtfulness of
your compositions" I shall again put down to
the account of ungovernable fury, and not complain of that either, as it leads your thoughts
to so desirable a result. And yet, to be candid,
I do complain of it after all; and only hope
that when you get these lines everything will
look brighter and more rose-coloured.

I can write but little about myself, or anything else, just now. If the dear God will only
grant me and all of us a happy Spring—then
everything will go well again, even letter-
writing. There's little I can say or do now, but
always keep on thinking. If only the dear God
would grant us a happy Spring. And because· I
don't want to go on repeating this in a letter, I
will to-day only make haste and answer your
questions. Do you mean that for a joke, what
you say about the Director-general of the sacred
music? or does it only sound so, without your
intending it? You must know that I don't get
the least thing for it but the title on paper, and
nobody knows whether I shall ever get anything
more. I neither have the right nor the wish

to interfere in anything that goes on, or does not go on, in the way of music in Berlin. This much only do I know from all my experiences, that you would find it very difficult to give the oratorio in a concert of your own—it is difficult to make the civilities requisite for inducing the chorus to sing, the money for getting the orchestra to play, and the unheard-of perfection which is necessary to make the public really interested ; therefore it's better that the Sing-Akademie should give it at their concerts, and you should conduct. Anyhow, you ought soon to communicate with Rungenhagen about it ; I would gladly save you the trouble and bother of a correspondence with that Society, if, on the one hand, I were not already utterly weary of them, and on the other did not know that my recommendation would more likely produce the opposite effect, if any at all ; because everything there is done in a sort of haphazard way, and according to that strange Berlin *je ne sais quoi,* by which nobody knows, nobody cares, but everybody rules, from the King down to the meanest porter and the pensioned drummer. As far as one can reasonably foresee, a letter from you to Rungenhagen would be the best thing at present ; especially if you can therein refer to your

conversation with Rellstab, and say something
about his having advised you, and so on.

But, as I have already said, business being
chiefly carried on in an unreasonable way there,
a different plan may perhaps be just as good—
for instance, if you happened to know one of
the managers, and could entrust the matter to
him. ·If all this doesn't suit you, and you want
me to write to him, then I shall have to do that
too, and everything else that I can, to please
you ; but, as I said before, I think I could then
answer for a failure, and their unbusiness-like and
unartist-like style of procedure is almost more
than I can stand. Forgive this philippic. I
suppose I shall be in the right, whatever the
newspapers say, good or bad. I am working
at the music for the "Midsummer Night's
Dream," with chorus, entr'actes, &c., and when
I have done that I shall also finish the choruses
for "Œdipus," which I have begun. I know next
to nothing about the "Tempest," so only a third
of those reports, if even that, has any foundation.

You want me to write about Berlioz ? A
subject like that is far too vast and full of detail ?
besides even as to his success or non-success,
his giving pleasure or not, there are so many
different opinions. In the autumn, when you
come here, I will tell you about it ; now if you

would only be very curious, and come a week sooner! Best remembrances to your wife from us both. Farewell, and may we have a happy meeting!

Your FELIX.

CHAPTER VIII.

SINCE the accession of King Frederic William
IV., who wanted to transplant Mendelssohn to
his capital, the latter had often wavered between
living at Berlin or at Leipsic. He was drawn to
Berlin by his promise, and to Leipsic by his inclinations. However, at the end of 1843 it was
decided that the whole family should move to
Berlin ; and under these circumstances I received
at Frankfort the flattering proposal that I should
undertake the direction of the Gewandhaus
Concerts during Mendelssohn's absence. Though
seeing very clearly that a temporary situation of
that sort would have its difficulties, and how
hazardous it would be to follow immediately
after, or rather act as substitute for, a conductor
who was worshipped to the degree that Mendelssohn was, I still thought I could not refuse ; for
since my marriage, I had been longing for some
regular, artistic occupation, such as my friend

had long wished me to have, and a more interesting one than that now offered me at Leipsic
could hardly be imagined.

So I crossed the Rubicon and the Fulda with
a light heart, and on the 23rd, arrived in Leipsic,
where a few hours afterwards, whilst my wife was
resting from the fatigues of the journey, I was
present with Mendelssohn and other friends at a
performance of " Samson," in St. Thomas's Church,
under the direction of Hauptmann. The peculiar
situation in which Felix and I stood towards
each other caused a slight *gêne* that evening, but
next day it entirely disappeared. He and David
came to see me early in the morning; in the
evening he accompanied us to a performance at
the theatre, supped with us afterwards in the
hotel, and was in such exuberant spirits, so gay
and genial and communicative, that I felt how
anxious he was to put everything on a smooth
footing.

He confessed to Cécile and David that at the
first meeting he had felt rather a pang at seeing
the person who was to fill the place he so loved
and gave up so unwillingly. But how little this
disturbed his confidence in me he proved, by
repeatedly telling me that it would not be impossible under certain conditions to fulfil the
promises he had made to the King, and still

retain his accustomed sphere of work at Leipsic.
He even initiated me so far into the secret as to
tell me the particulars of the conditions, and
to beg for my candid opinion on the subject. I
could only advise him to agree to them.

He also gladly volunteered to play in the first
concert which I conducted, and which took place
on the 1st of October. He played his G minor
Concerto, which David allowed me to conduct,
although it was his duty to conduct all solos with
orchestral accompaniment. It was the first time
I heard the Concerto with orchestra, though I
had known it in Paris. It made a most favourable
impression on the public that he should thus ini-
tiate my first appearance at the conductor's desk
by taking a part in the concert, and it was
thought to do honour to both of us.

A few days afterwards he went off to Berlin,
without his family, to conduct the first performance of the "Midsummer Night's Dream."
I followed on the 11th with David and the
clever good-natured Niels Gade, who had just
come to Leipsic for the first time. The young
prodigy Joachim also could not resist the temptation of going to hear this latest work of Mendelssohn's. On the 14th it was given for the
first time in the "New Palace." Mendelssohn
joined us at dinner at the "Einsiedler" in

Potsdam, after the rehearsal ; he seemed very well satisfied, and we had a most lively and pleasant meeting.

The performance of the " Midsummer Night's Dream " enchanted me. The actors managed their parts capitally, though the lovely and popular Charlotte von Hagen would have been more in her sphere in a drawing-room or ballet than in the part of the elfin Ariel. The comic scenes were irresistibly amusing, and the *mise en scène*, especially the children's ballet, was quite poetic. But above all this, even above the great Shakespeare's verses, did I enjoy the wonderfully lovely music ; that alone would be enough to stamp Mendelssohn for ever as one of the cleverest of Tone-masters and Tone-poets. The band played to perfection ; Felix had had eleven rehearsals, and the result showed what was possible with means like these under the direction of such a conductor.

It is characteristic of Mendelssohn's views of things that he should have been very much excited after the performance, and this from a twofold cause. It had been arranged, according to his wish, that the whole thing, with the entr'actes, should be played without any pause whatsoever, as in his opinion this was indispensable for the proper effect. Nevertheless, not only was a long

pause introduced, but it was made use of to
offer all kinds of refreshments to the people in
the front rows belonging to the Court, so that a
full half-hour was taken up with loud talking
and moving about, whilst the rest of the audience,
who were quite as much invited, though perhaps
only tolerated, were sitting in discomfort, and
had to beguile the time as best they could. This
disregard of artistic considerations, as well as
common civility, so enraged Mendelssohn that he
hardly took any notice of all the fine things that
we had to say to him.

A few days after I had returned to Leipsic,
Felix also came back there. Musical life was in
full flow: Gade gave us a new symphony, Schumann brought out his "Paradise and the Peri"
for the first time, Mendelssohn played at a chamber
concert, and we performed Bach's Triple Concerto
once more, Clara Schumann taking the first part
in it. Mendelssohn's relations with that great
artist had always been based on the most chival-
rous affection, and I well remember a charming
little incident illustrative of this, which occurred
at a *matinée* at the house of our dear friend
Bendemann the painter.

A large number of friends had been invited to
hear Mendelssohn, Clara Schumann amongst them.
He played Beethoven's great F minor Sonata

("Appassionata"); at the end of the Andante he let the final chord of the diminished seventh ring on for a long time, as if he wanted to impress it very forcibly on all present; then he quietly got up, and turning to Madame Schumann, said "You must play the Finale." She strongly protested. Meanwhile all were awaiting the issue with the utmost tension, the chord of the diminished seventh hovering over our heads all the time like the sword of Damocles. I think it was chiefly the nervous, uncomfortable feeling of this unresolved discord which at last moved Madame Schumann to yield to Mendelssohn's entreaties and give us the Finale. The end was worthy of the beginning, and if the order had been reversed it would no doubt have been just as fine.

The King of Saxony was present at one of the first of the Gewandhaus Concerts which I conducted. Mendelssohn arranged a great soirée in the Gewandhaus Concert-room in honour of the Grand Duchess Hélène, and also played to her on the organ. He was busy just then with a four-hand arrangement of the "Midsummer Night's Dream" music, and I used to try it over with him as he finished each part. He put off his departure for Berlin as long as possible, evidently finding it very hard to separate himself from a circle which had become so dear to him.

In one of his very affectionate letters to me he once * suddenly asked : " Do you really think we could ever quarrel ? I think not." As far as I was concerned it seemed to me impossible. But, with a sorrowful heart, I must here mention the fact, that it did come to a *brouille* between us, arising from social, and not from personal, susceptibilities. I think we were both in the wrong, but no angry words passed between us, and certainly the matter would soon have been smoothed over if he had not gone to Berlin in the beginning of December. However, it put an end to our correspondence, even though Mendelssohn's feelings towards me remained unchanged; I heard this often enough, sooner or later, from mutual friends, as well as from his wife. In fact, I have just now, quite by chance, come across a letter which he wrote to his old friend Professor Hildebrandt at Düsseldorf, on the 1st of October, 1847, five weeks before his death, and which I cannot quote, because my doing so would be mistaken for the strongest self-praise. But I look upon the cessation of my intercourse with that wonderful man during his last years, even though it was only an external separation, as one of the greatest losses which I have sustained in my agitated life.

---

* See *ante,* page 66.—*Ed.*

On my way to Düsseldorf, where I had accepted the post of musical director, I came to Leipsic on the 11th of November, 1847, a week after Mendelssohn's death. Cécile received me with tearful eyes, wonderfully calm, and her lovely features transfigured with grief. She told me that even during his last illness Felix had often spoken of me and of my appointment to Düsseldorf with the greatest sympathy. In the evening there was a concert at the Gewandhaus to his memory. "The saddest thing," says George Sand somewhere, "after the death of a beloved being, is the empty place at table." I had exactly the same feeling during the concert. There were the orchestra, the chorus, the audience, which for so many years had been inspired by Mendelssohn; they made their music and played and sang—and only a few days before they had followed his corpse to the church. I could hardly listen to the music—his last song, most touchingly sung by Madame Frege, is all that I remember of it. Indeed it seemed to me impossible that there should so soon again be music in that Gewandhaus Concert-room; but life must go on as usual, and the bereaved must again assemble for the accustomed musical feast!

A few years later, during a short stay in Berlin, I was one day dining with Mendelssohn's widow, surrounded by her charming children, and could not help feeling deeply affected; the ingenuous bantering prattle of the children, the graceful, gentle way in which Cécile tried to check their high spirits, nearly overcame me. How much happiness was lost to him who had been taken from us—how much happiness those who were left behind had been robbed of!

Again after some years I returned for a few days to my native town. I had heard very sad accounts of the state of health of Mendelssohn's widow, who was then staying in Frankfort, and I feared the worst. It was on the 25th of September, 1853, I went to the house of Cécile's family and rung the well-known bell, which had so often answered to my touch when I went prepared for happy times. In a few minutes Mendelssohn's mother-in-law, Madame Jeanrenaud, burst out of her room and opened the door for me. She was expecting Cécile's brother-in-law. "Oh, it is *you*, dear Mr. Hiller," she said in a gasping voice, with that frightful calm which often comes from despair—"I have just lost my daughter!"

CONCLUSION.

THE mass of the public are in general not ill-pleased when either great poets, or great composers, fare somewhat badly. People pity their fate, but the misery which they have endured invests them with a certain interest. The outward radiance which shone around Goethe certainly procured him numerous opponents, and the advantageous circumstances which surrounded Mendelssohn from his birth are by many still looked on as blemishes.

" Le génie c'est la faim," said a Russian diplomatist to me one day. This absurd witticism meant nothing more than that a small amount of starvation is very wholesome diet for genius. But even that is false. Talent may be spurred on by it to the energy which is necessary for its development; but genius works by the force of nature, and the material· difficulties with which it has to struggle are like rocks in the bed of a mighty stream; it dashes over them, making lovely waterfalls as it goes.

The struggle for the bare necessaries of life may be hard enough, but in itself it has no special merit. It is only the instinct of self-preservation which compels the mere labourer to work, and though the struggle may be more painful when the head is called into action instead of the hands, it is certainly not more meritorious. A second kind of struggle is that against prejudice, against want of understanding, against jealousy, or whatever all such fine things may be called; but what champion of light can be spared this? More or less, everybody has to fight these battles, some sooner, some later, and in the midst of this second struggle it is far harder to preserve the desire for creating, and the power of willing, than it is to resist the first one. It is certainly very unfortunate, when, as often happens, both struggles are combined. Whether the increased admiration which is paid to anyone who has made his way in the face of want, is perfectly justified, remains to be seen. Anyhow, it certainly depends very much on the manner in which he fights.

Perhaps a stronger, because a more independent, force of will is needed to produce great things out of wealth than out of poverty. Who

has not known men of remarkable gifts, varied
knowledge, overflowing eloquence, who—I will
not say by the force of genius, but by superior
gifts of mind—would have been able to produce
great things for the public benefit, if the world
had not gone "too well" with them? When
people bring riches and position into the world
with them, all that remains to be acquired of
this world's goods is fame, and it is not everyone who is born to that. Contact with the
public, to say the least of it, is unpleasant—it
is like the wind which fans the large flame, but
extinguishes the small one—and the thankless
work which even genius has to do, the self-sacrifice
which she requires on so many sides, frightens
many away, whilst the feeling of duty which
demands that something should be done for the
benefit of society, if one has the stuff for it, is
much less often found than could be wished for
the honour of mankind. Therefore, when an
artist like Mendelssohn devotes his whole
strength to giving even his smallest songs that
perfection which always hovered before him as
his ideal, when he strains his full power and
knowledge to advance all that is best in his art
on every side, he deserves no less acknowledg-
ment because he happens to be in a position
free from all material cares, than if he were

compelled to wait for the reward of his work in order to pay his debts. Or is that preference for misery the unexpressed feeling, which in fact ought never to be expressed, that it is too much of a good thing when outward prosperity is united to the happiness of possessing the poetic creative faculty? Such a preference must surely arise from error. The satisfaction of a man who forcibly conquers mean cares must surely be much greater than that of one who never felt them.

Be this as it may, the spectacle of those spiritual warriors, who, like the heroes in Kaulbach's "Battle of the Huns," are lifted above the earth, and strive for victory in the clouds, is at any rate more gratifying than that of those who fight on the earth and raise clouds of dust. They themselves are works of art; their bright forms are beautiful, apart from the palmbranches which wave before them; and one ought to feel the proudest pleasure that fate succeeds, though but seldom, in bringing forward a thoroughly free man.

Felix Mendelssohn was a bright being of this nature. Gifts of genius were in him united to the most careful culture, tenderness of heart to sharpness of understanding, playful facility in everything that he attempted, to powerful energy

for the highest tasks. A noble feeling of gratitude penetrated his pure heart at every good
thing which fell to his lot. This pious disposition,
pious in the best sense of the word, was the secret
of his constant readiness to give pleasure and to
show active sympathy.

Were it conceivable that all his works should
perish, the remembrance of his poetic nature
would alone suffice to afford the German public
the great satisfaction of thinking that such a being
was born in their midst, and bloomed and ripened
there.

How gloriously the Greeks would have
honoured and praised him as a chosen favourite
of Apollo and the Muses! For "all the highest
things are free gifts from the gods."

INDEX